Making a Difference in the Classroom

Strategies That Connect with Students

SANDRA J. BALLI

ROWMAN & LITTLEFIELD EDUCATION
Lanham • New York • Toronto • Plymouth, UK

Published in the United States of America
by Rowman & Littlefield Education
A Division of Rowman & Littlefield Publishers, Inc.
A wholly owned subsidary of The Rowman & Littlefield Publishing Group, Inc.
4501 Forbes Boulevard, Suite 200, Lanham, Maryland 20706
www.rowmaneducation.com

Estover Road
Plymouth PL6 7PY
United Kingdom

British Library Cataloguing in Publication Information Available

Library of Congress Cataloging-in-Publication Data

Balli, Sandra J.
  Making a difference in the classroom : strategies that connect with students / Sandra J.
Balli.
     p. cm.
  Includes bibliographical references.
  ISBN 978-1-60709-034-2 (cloth : alk. paper) — ISBN 978-1-60709-035-9 (pbk. : alk. pa-
per) — ISBN 978-1-60709-036-6 (electronic)
  1. Teaching. 2. Effective teaching. 3. Teacher-student relationships. 4. Classroom envi-
ronment. I. Title.
  LB1025.3.B34 2009

With admiration for teachers—
you make a difference

Contents

Acknowledgments

Writing a book is a large undertaking, one that is never accomplished in isolation. My appreciation goes to the many people whose wisdom, over time, has helped shape my thinking about teaching and learning.

Special thanks to my chairperson, Anita Oliver, who, over a sounding-board lunch one day, remarked, "Why don't you write a book?" I am grateful as well to our dean, Ed Boyatt, for his patient encouragement and financial support.

With deep gratitude and recognition to David Berliner, who graciously agreed to write the foreword. His important research on the pursuit of excellence in teaching has inspired me and countless other teachers for more than two decades.

There is no match for the reality check on classroom life that K–12 teachers can offer teacher educators. My sincere appreciation to Erin Kurtz, Cameron Fraser, and Jennifer Castillo, who model excellence in education and whose careful feedback and insightful comments contributed enormously to the lessons and clarity embodied in this book.

My heartfelt gratitude extends as well to those in higher education, Roger Johnson and Bill Ayers, and to William Glasser. They each offered a great deal to the focus of this book with their intuitive and helpful suggestions. Thank you also goes to David Ajao, my research assistant, whose constructive ideas and listening ear encouraged me to begin writing.

With profound appreciation to Tom Koerner, Maera Stratton, Lynn Weber, Bruce Owens, and others at Rowman & Littlefield Publishing whose professional competence, editorial suggestions, and skill have been incredibly valuable.

Thank you to the students, listed by pseudonym throughout the book, whose vignettes about excellent teachers illustrate what making a difference in the classroom is all about. As the recipients of all that teachers orchestrate, students are eminently positioned to understand its impact.

And finally, to my family—my husband, Don; our children and their spouses, Karen, Scott, Kevin, and Meaghan; our grandchildren, Megan, Casey, Claire, Jack, and Ava; my parents, Charles and Beverly; and my mother-in-law, Estelle—you each bless my life immeasurably.

Foreword

My research with expert teachers taught me that many of the experts we studied were not good mentor teachers. Although quite wonderful to watch in the classroom, some of our extraordinary teachers were relatively inarticulate about the reasons they behaved in certain ways. They could not articulate the reasons they engaged in certain instructional acts or tell us why they made certain statements to students. Their classroom behavior seemed so well suited for the subject they taught, the lesson they were presenting, the kinds of students they had, and the problems they encountered. Their interpersonal skills seemed to be wonderful as well: warm, sensible, respectful, fair, and so matter-of-fact they made teaching look easy. But many of them could not tell us why they did what they did.

So it is with the greatest of pleasure that I introduce this book by an expert teacher, an expert mentor of teachers, and one of the most analytic and clear communicators about what it takes to become an extraordinary teacher. I think that Sandy Balli has nailed it. Her advice and tutorials are compatible with the research on teacher expertise but much more vivid and lively because she knows classroom life so well. This is a perfect book for new teachers and struggling teachers because Balli has taught, is able to analyze her teaching, and has exceptional skills in communicating the wisdom that is inherent in her practice. She is an excellent example of a reflective practitioner.

I was struck by how well Balli understands the emotional ties that are capable of bringing great joy to both teachers and students alike. With her sensitive emotional antennae, she also sees how life can be made more difficult for students when their teacher is unable or unwilling to learn the skills or make the commitment to students that is characteristic of our nation's best teachers. She is well aware that both teachers and students are imperfect people with intricate and fragile human natures who must learn to coexist in classrooms. She uses her experience to help teachers design a pleasant and high-performing learning community, even when one or the other sees the tasks set by outside forces as undesirable, such as overreliance on high-stakes tests for accountability.

Balli reminds us that successful learning communities are not so different from successful societies. So the kinds of relationships she tries to foster between teachers and their students are precisely the kinds of relationships we hope would characterize the interactions between members of a successful democratic society. The civility, seriousness of purpose, and joy in the classrooms she most admires and teaches us to create is what we hope will characterize the lives of all our citizenry.

I could not help thinking that John Dewey lives in this book. I certainly felt his presence throughout. Dewey—and now Balli—reminds us that school should not be thought of as preparation for life but is, in fact, life itself. Both understand that learning in communities is the preferred mode of instruction for achievement as well as preparation for living in a democracy, that respect for teachers and their knowledge comes out of the respect shown by teachers for their students, and that real-life projects engage students more than do most paper-and-pencil, abstract tasks.

Balli says, as Dewey might have, that allowing students to have some choices in what curriculum they study is a good way to uncover hidden interests. She rightly notes that a little room in the curriculum for student choice, at any grade level, gives students more of a sense of responsibility for their own learning, a desire to accomplish something worthwhile, and a feeling of control over their products and outcomes. Note how radical this thought is in our times. In recent years we have seen the government sponsoring scripted curriculum. We saw state content standards created but failed to notice how those standards also standardize exactly what is to be learned. And we witnessed how high-stakes testing programs narrow the curriculum to that which is to be on the test.

In the midst of all these powerful contemporary forces, Balli makes the case for some student choice of the curriculum to be studied. Her experience and explanations for her teaching philosophy are so wonderfully out of sync with many of the classroom practices we see today. Hers is the voice of a successful teacher and teacher-educator who shares with us a vision of teaching for student learning that is admirable.

Balli hopes to influence teachers in a way similar to Jonathan Kozol's recent book *Letters to a Young Teacher*. Both say to render unto the state what you must but keep the idealism that brought you into teaching at the forefront of your interactions with students. Both Balli and Kozol urge teachers to keep in mind those teachers they admired, those who influenced their lives.

Balli's ideas are also compatible with the philosopher Nell Noddings, who keeps reminding us about the importance of an ethic of caring in education. Balli, like Noddings, sees a system that overly values the instrumental value of education and doesn't recognize often enough education's contribution to the development of students' emotional security and the promotion of excellence in the work that students must accomplish.

Balli's writing about respect and her emphasis on caring by teachers, themes that run throughout the book, make the point quite clearly that classrooms form personalities based primarily on these relationships. She notes that respect and caring for the hardest-to-like or most difficult-to-handle students, of which there are always too many, signals the way teachers will be treated in return by their other students. In addition, communicating respect and demonstrating an ethic of caring for students does much to defuse the possibility of cultural clashes in a classroom or a school.

Balli's advice about how to be an exceptional teacher would be inadequate if she only dealt with the emotional relationships in a classroom. But she goes on, as she should, to talk about the commitments to the teaching profession and to student learning that are always significant factors in the lives of exemplary teachers. If a teacher has the will to become an exemplary instructor of subject matter content, Balli's advice about how to do this is creative and practical.

Hers is the voice of experience and common sense in describing ways to learn what students already know and what they have trouble learning in order to plan lessons that allow for diversity in how curriculum is learned and how it is assessed. She promotes active learning and the integration of real-life experiences into the classroom, again updating the voice of John Dewey for an

era that badly needs caring, competent, communitarian teachers as role models for our youth. I have no doubt that the advice contained in *Making a Difference in the Classroom* can actually make a difference in the classrooms of
our students and their teachers.

David C. Berliner
Regents' Professor
Mary Lou Fulton College of Education
Arizona State University

Introduction

When I was in third grade, my teacher, Mrs. Houghton, assigned our class oral reports on science topics of our choice. For the first time, I was required to stand in front of the class and talk—scary stuff for an eight-year-old. Apprehensive but undaunted, I made plans to report on what happens in the body during a heart attack. The year was 1955, and *Life* magazine had chronicled President Eisenhower's near fatal heart attack with numerous medical illustrations. Carefully cutting a selection of illustrations and mounting them on poster board, I diligently prepared what I would say.

On the day of our reports, I faced the class and described a heart attack step-by-step, pointing on cue to my visual aids with confidence. Mrs. Houghton listened; even the kids listened. Standing there, in front of the class, wasn't so scary after all. Later that day, Mrs. Houghton took me aside. With hands clasped loosely in front of her plain cotton dress, she leaned in toward me, smiled, and candidly remarked that I would make a good teacher. In third grade, I'd not yet considered a real grown-up job, but her comment sparked my imaginings as I fancied day after day of explaining other things besides heart attacks.

That afternoon, when my mother gathered me and my belongings from school, Mrs. Houghton caught my mother's attention and described my oral report to her, repeating that she believed I would make a good teacher. Even at eight years old, I grasped, on some level, that this conversation, between two important adults in my life, held significance.

I don't know if I decided on that very day, but the encounter with my third-grade teacher captured my dreams and charted my course into teaching. Mrs. Houghton never knew how she imprinted my life, yet I can envision her delight and humble acknowledgment had she known that my thirty-year journey into teaching and teacher education could be traced, in part, to her comment on one ordinary day in her classroom. Such is the subtle yet profound influence of a good teacher.

FAST-FORWARD

Years after my encounter with Mrs. Houghton, I paused at the beginning of a new semester to survey the university students filing into my introductory teacher education course. All told, I would see nearly 150 students that first week. As the mix of young men and women chose seats in the tiered auditorium, they greeted me with reserved smiles, cursory nods, and quizzical faces. I wondered about their journey to this place. Clearly, each one traveled a unique route, and, having discarded other professional roads, they chose to study teaching.

What were they thinking on this first day? Teach me to teach? Or did most suppose that they already knew how to teach? After all, they had encountered a wide enough spectrum of teachers in their schooling—kind and mean, inspiring and boring, equitable and unjust—to inform what they did and did not want to do in their own classrooms someday. More than likely many occupied space in my classroom just waiting to get through and commence their real lives as teachers. I suppressed an audible sigh.

As their teacher, I was certain of one thing: these students came with a vision of themselves as teachers, formed largely from observing their own teachers and selecting suitable teacher qualities here and there, like bits of marble for a mosaic. Would I systematically chip away at their vision, replacing it with burdensome requirements and technical minutiae layered one upon another like so many building blocks? To be sure, students were enrolled in a foundations course, and building blocks lay in abundant supply here.

Looking out at these expectant students, I wondered if the essential but grueling tasks required to build their way toward teacher certification would eclipse their broader vision of teaching until it faded like a veiled dream. This thought occurred to me at the beginning of each school year and never ceased to jar me like the block wall I hoped my students would avoid.

I decided at the outset to capture and honor my students' visions by revitalizing all the "Mrs. Houghtons" from their past experiences. After all, like me, these students had chosen teaching for a career, and they did so for a reason. Somewhere, along the way, students encountered a representation of excellence, a dynamic representation of what they hoped to become.

And so I invited the students to consider their excellent teachers, from kindergarten through college, and to select a specific memory still etched in their minds. No one asked me what I meant by "excellent" teacher. They knew. Spontaneously and without consulting with one another about their choices, my 148 students penned an encounter with an excellent teacher.

READING AND REFLECTING

Reading my students' encounters with teachers compelled me to reflect on my own teaching journey. I remembered my first blundering attempts to forge relationships with students both younger and older, the struggle to find my way through simply delivering content to partnering with students in a learning community, and the ongoing quest to understand who I was as a teacher and to recognize my unique contribution to students. What had I learned as a teacher from experiences and observations through all grade levels over three decades? What had I learned from reading 148 student encounters with teachers? Could the lessons and teacher and student perspectives be laced together in some meaningful way? It soon became clear that there was a story to tell.

ABOUT THIS BOOK

This book is about teaching and the life, energy, substance, hope, and determination that excellent teachers bring to the rhythm of classrooms every day, year in and year out. Ultimately, schooling, despite its external pressures and cynics, comes down to students, to what happens in the classroom, and to the person who orchestrates it—the teacher.

The book packages experiences and lessons from classroom life through the voice of teachers, both mine and others. Likewise, the book offers a diorama of encounters with teachers, sprinkled here and there, to illustrate classroom life through the voice of students. Knitting teacher and student perspectives together, the book intends to inspire teachers and those who are learning to teach with universal insights drawn from elementary school, middle school, high school, and college.

The book is organized into three parts. Part I focuses on teacher–student relationships, the critical foundation that supports and nourishes respectful classroom life. Part II illuminates how teachers finesse the substance and action of classrooms, blending endless elements and decisions into a vibrant learning community. Part III probes the inestimable worth of teachers, as diverse individuals, with unique talents to offer as gifts for students to unwrap and experience day after day.

The book may evoke emotion, a feeling of affirmation, and a call for introspection. In the process, students of teaching will affirm why they chose the teaching profession, practicing teachers will affirm why they stay, and those who observe education will see what it takes to be an excellent teacher. For anyone interested not only in the practical elements of excellent teaching but also in the aura that swirls around teachers who make it look effortless, you may find the best of yourself somewhere among the coming pages. I hope so.

I

BUILDING RELATIONSHIPS

Teachers and students coexist in classrooms of imperfect people with intricate and fragile human natures. This reality presents a considerable challenge for human interaction; teacher to student, student to teacher, and student to student. The hundreds of encounters among this tangle of people are significant, sometimes pivotal, impacting classroom life and relationships in profound ways.

Teachers have long known that classrooms are a breeding ground for an assortment of irritations as well as affirmations, indifferences as well as connections, and misunderstandings as well as harmony. Along the way, human emotions and interactions mingle and merge, often in unpredictable or unintentional ways, but all contribute variously to strong or strained relationships among those who abide together in classrooms.

As the persons responsible for classroom life, teachers hold the key to setting the tone and charting relationships. Understandably, in the daily hum of classroom discourse, teachers often go about the work of schooling unaware that their particular habits—their passing encounters or purposeful interactions—sear remarkable images into the minds of students for good or ill. Because relationships are the fundamental bedrock of classroom life with far-reaching consequences, a closer look at the principles and nuances involved in building good relationships is worth our time and attention.

1

Respect

■ There was a boy in our class who had coke-bottle glasses and buck-teeth, but no one made fun of him. I believe this was because our teacher treated him with respect. The boy was really cool—or at least I thought he was, and as far as I remember so did everyone else. I believe he was given a chance to really develop despite his looks. Most kids would have been making fun of him, and the typical teacher would just let this kind of treatment slide. Our teacher would not and did not let this happen. (Becky)

ODD DUCK OUT

From time to time I watch a raft of ducks as they waddle in and out of a nearby pond. One of the ducks limps slowly and awkwardly behind the others, unable to keep pace, noticeably disadvantaged by an injury apparent through several wing feathers that stick out at odd angles. The isolated duck, consistently shunned by the other ducks, limps his solitary way from pond to grass and back again like a perpetual Forrest Gump without an advocate to champion him as a worthwhile member of the duck community.

Schoolchildren can be a lot like these ducks, isolating other children who are different, flawed in some fabricated way that makes them unworthy of acceptance. Flaws can take on any number of unfortunate labels, like coke-bottle glasses, but the result is familiar to the sitting duck: loneliness, humiliation, and pain. Truth is, we all have oddities—anomalous flaws we seek to disguise hoping others won't notice or, worse yet, point out for unwanted attention.

I recall dodging a steady round of teasing in second grade for looking like a "boy" simply because my mother had given me a very short summer haircut that didn't grow out until November. My smiling, boyish-looking second-grade picture belies the embarrassment that coursed through me when singled out on a daily basis for childish taunts. Although such ridicule creeps into classroom and playground discourse with an offhanded comment, a band of unchecked children who ratchet up the ridicule define a routine, almost normal way of interacting with an outcast student, a virtual captive in the school yard and classroom.

Consider the disparity between a classroom outcast and an outcast in other settings where an unaccepted person generally has a choice: endure intolerance or leave. The alienated student, with little choice, dreads each school day, praying to awaken with a real fever or imagined illness to avoid the inevitable. Ostracized students can dwell dejected in classrooms if not for the life-changing impact of teachers who model and cultivate respect.

Respect begins with an unwavering commitment to all students and springs from a teacher's deliberate choice to breed an environment of acceptance and shepherd students to breathe its contagious atmosphere like a serene, fresh breeze. In the opening vignette, classmates considered the boy with coke-bottle glasses and buckteeth not only worthwhile but also "cool"— an immensely favorable characterization. He didn't need protection because his peers accepted him as if he had perfect vision and naturally straight lily-white teeth. Such a classroom, deliberately fashioned and saturated with acceptance and worth, feels fundamentally different from one in which a teacher must regularly admonish students to refrain from demeaning comments.

■ Obviously, she really wanted to be a teacher. She treated every student as a special individual with his or her own talents and contributions. She planned opportunities for each student to be creative. Everyone respected her, not just her students but her colleagues as well. She didn't demand this respect; she earned it. (Margaret)

For a teacher, it takes grace, persistence, and unselfish regard to embrace all students freely and warmly with their mix of foibles and deficiencies, and it takes courage to furtively redirect students who designate odd-duck status to any classmate. Teacher energy is well spent in cultivating the classroom soil to harvest each student's unique capacities, celebrating those with thanksgiving as useful and necessary to the classroom community.

Fortunately, our son, Kevin, had such a teacher. Kevin endured petty teasing at an elementary school basketball game when, momentarily disoriented, he ran down the court to the opponent's side, sinking the ball and scoring for the opposing team. About the same time, his discerning teacher recognized and enlisted Kevin's natural ability to play the accordion; and thus began his miniconcerts in the classroom with admiring students clustered around him, the offending basketball game long forgotten.

RESPECT FOR STUDENT CONTRIBUTIONS

Interaction among students and between teachers and students is a central feature of classroom life worthy of careful regard and insight. Students who feel valued as individuals are liberated to offer their budding talents and untested contributions in class, secure that these matter to the teacher and, if received with respect, will similarly matter to the whole class. This way of doing classroom business takes teacher commitment, but the satisfying memories linger long for students.

My high school English teacher recognized the rights of students to be respected, not treated as inferior or less important. He promoted discussion and exchange of ideas. He fostered an atmosphere conducive to expression. I trusted him completely with my education; he recognized me as an individual and someone with a contribution to make. (Mariah)

Teachers regularly endure a time crunch when even a few minutes to complete a lesson concept are essential, and harried teachers may succumb to the fallacy that content coverage trumps time allotted for student contributions. Unfortunately, the time crunch that clamps teachers like a mouse in a trap restricts our broader goals and tricks us into believing that we have certainly allowed adequate opportunity for student input. Preoccupied with scripted lessons, we may be unmindful of a student's inclination to challenge a concept, offer an insight, or ask a simple question.

Years ago, I received a note from a student stating her burning desire that I respect her opinions. I was stunned. With plummeting teacher efficacy, I sifted through my memory, class after class, but, self-righteously, could not recall a time when I had not respected a student's opinion. But fooled like the unsuspecting mouse looking for cheese, I had to face the truth that during an otherwise important lesson, I had not listened with respect or validated her contribution. A careless moment, perhaps, but I determined to give more thoughtful consideration to this important issue and to set about altering lesson routines lest opportunities for validation be dismissed but remembered by students with stinging reality. Admittedly, avoiding the time-crunch mousetrap is easier said than done.

Although students of any age want their opinions respected and taken seriously, adolescent students view themselves with a tangled mix of bravado and self-loathing. Often, adolescents are more vulnerable and hesitant than younger students to contribute ideas that might be prone to dismissal. Despite the quality of contributed ideas, teachers who approach students with interest and engagement jump-start them to play with new ideas as they refine and improve their contributions with practice.

■ I think the thing that stands out most in my mind was that he respected our opinions. He actually thought his students knew something, and he placed a high value on our thoughts. Too often teachers think their job is to know everything and that their way of thinking is the only correct way. It seemed to me that he was less concerned about the factual information we retained and more concerned with validating our answers. (April)

A belief that "he placed a high value on our thoughts" reveals a relationship of deep mutual trust with a teacher. Imagine the big issues that could be peeled back and examined within a trusted relationship. Imagine the possibilities in classrooms across the country where teachers who model respect are trusted to guide awakening minds and citizens.

Teachers who desire to impact the outside world do so not by pressing a prescribed agenda but by their consistent influence and openness to the diverse students who journey through their classrooms year after year and venture out to make the world a better place. Initially, teachers and students create their own unique world, a fortressed classroom society with teacher and student citizens. If respect governs the society—if differing opinions are heard, investigated, and valued—the classroom evolves into a microcosm of hope and possibility for the future of the larger society, fed by ripples amassing into waves of habitual, respectful interactions among those of like and unlike minds.

GROWN-UP TREATMENT

■ She talked to her students at an adult level. We never felt stupid or like we were being talked down to. She treated us like other people instead of students she could walk on. She respected us and treated us like adults. (Melanie)

Taking students seriously uplifts them to a more esteemed position than a name on a classroom roster or an occupant in a cafeteria lunch line. Teachers who validate student contributions elevate students to a respected level, almost akin, in a young mind, to being an adult—a secure position that eases the considerable insecurities of growing up.

Some teachers may be uncomfortable with the notion of elevating students in this way. It may seem oddly out of sync to teachers accustomed to a draconian line that distinguishes all teachers from all students. They wonder whether granting adult respect will blur the line and threaten the authority of the teacher, who, after all, is the one in charge and responsible for all that transpires in a classroom.

What do students mean when they speak of "adult" treatment? Do they covet an adult moniker? Eventually, of course, but most young people aren't looking to replace backpacks with briefcases sooner than necessary. I suspect it has more to do with the disparity between the way adults talk to kids and the way adults talk to other adults.

Picture teachers who converse with students in halfhearted, half-listening, or, worse yet, demeaning ways, then abruptly alter their demeanor, attitude, and words to converse with adults who happen by the classroom. Curt then courteous. Translation? Adults are worthy of respectful speech and polite attention, and students are not. For students, it must be refreshing to interact with teachers who treat all students with the same courtesy afforded the adults who move about the school.

■ On a typical day, we discussed not only plays, poems, literature, and vocabulary but also daily issues. The great thing was that he treated us like adults, even equals. He never yelled at any of us for being immature; rather, he respected us, and we respected him. Every day I learned something new from him, a down-to-earth fellow who is incredibly intelligent, well liked, and respected—any of his students would agree. (Erin)

I visited a middle school classroom one spring to observe a mathematics lesson but learned a broader lesson in dignity and adult respect. The teacher identified his students as "ladies and gentlemen" as if referring to honored guests at an important event. The event was a math class, but it could well have been a king's reception. When the students answered and even when they did not or when he wanted their attention, he requested it with the same dignified, subdued "ladies and gentlemen" in words and tone. The students responded in kind with decorum and cooperation. "Ladies and gentlemen, please refer to the problem on the board" may sound quaint, like a provincial classroom greeting; nevertheless, respectful words appeared, to me, to resonate better with these students than a brash "hey you kids, get to work." The key here is not so much the specific words he used to address the students but rather the tone of voice and attitude that underscored the words.

■ She cared for and respected her students as young adults. She addressed each of us as "Ms. Smith" or "Mr. Jones." (Faith)

Ron Clark (2004a, 2004b), a Disney Teacher of the Year recipient, impacted his students in an inner-city Harlem school showing genuine interest in their lives and modeling adultlike respect. He surprised and dazzled his students with field trips to New York museums and plays, dignifying them as young adults yet indulging in kidlike fun with them on the playground. Clark suggests that teachers cannot underestimate the respect they will earn by showing kindhearted consideration. His far-reaching influence guided his at-risk students to attain heights of possibility heretofore considered improbable.

RESPECTFUL LISTENING

■ My ninth-grade art teacher taught commercial design, something I was not really interested in but took anyway. He motivated me to do

some good work at a time when I couldn't get motivated to do anything. Not study, not learn, not anything. What sticks out in my mind
is that he treated us like adults, well, at least not like children. He
talked with us like he knew we could understand him, and he always
listened to us with respect. (Olivia)

When diligent teachers attend to the business of teaching, unzipping lessons and activities to lure student involvement, they can easily and understandably forget to listen. Teachers need to not only listen to the words
students say but also be equally attuned to what students don't say but convey
more significantly through their facial expression and body language.

I recognized the obvious value of facial expression and body language
when a television camera shut me off from these nonverbal cues of deeper
meaning. In the mid-1980s, producers at the ABC affiliate in Dayton, Ohio,
invited me to appear regularly on their afternoon news broadcast. For the next
four years, as a teacher and home economist, I appeared every Tuesday to discuss a hot topic in nutrition, parenting, and the like.

The format included a short presentation followed by a live question-and-
answer call-in from the television audience, an exchange that proved exhilarating at times and unnerving at others. On the upside, viewers who found my
comments useful shared their gratitude in letters I received from time to time.
On the downside, viewers were blocked from asking follow-up questions, and,
of course, I couldn't see them, so I had no way of gauging their response
through facial expression or body language. It was impossible to know if I had
met a questioner's needs with sensitivity and respect or if the broader audience understood what I hoped to convey.

Back in the classroom, teachers have an advantage afforded by scanning a
classroom of students whose expressions and body language typically can't hide
what they really think. Nevertheless, it is still easy to miss something. Recently,
a teacher shared his eye-opening experience in planning a field trip with two
other teachers. The plan called for the teachers to accompany their combined
group of sixty third, fourth, and fifth graders on an exhilarating overnight trip.
As plans were finalized, the spirited teachers met with their students.

Buzzing on and on with a slew of stories and details, the teachers outlined
their grand itinerary. Meanwhile, the students' body language bore a decided
lack of enthusiasm. Finally, noticing their low energy and apprehensive

expressions, one of the teachers asked the students why they weren't more excited. One student timidly raised her hand and asked, "Will there be bathrooms there?" With much on their agenda, the teachers had misread what mattered most to the students. The students cared little about the fiesta of sights planned for the trip. They first wanted reassurance and respect for their basic needs.

■ The year I had him for biology, he was awarded teacher of the year for my school. What I remember most about him was his caring nature; his number one priority was making kids feel comfortable and respected. Once I was upset by another teacher and needed to talk to someone—he took the time out to really listen to me, but not only that—he was on my side (a strange occurrence for me). (Bridget)

Treating students with consideration, listening to them, reading their nonverbal cues, and relating to them with adultlike respect does not demean a teacher or result in a loss of real or perceived authority. Rather, by demonstrating respect for students, teachers demonstrate the essential nature of self-respect and personal dignity.

RESPECTING THE DISRESPECTFUL

Teachers who inspire know that teaching is like cultivating a garden and those who would have nothing to do with thorns must never attempt to gather flowers.

—Author unknown

■ She was interested in every student, even the ones who acted up and were class distractions. She treated us as people with brains and intelligence. (Kara)

It seems doable, even edifying, to treat naturally well-behaved and respectful students in kind. Students who have been raised in families or cultures that prize respect generally carry that same demeanor into the classroom. My students from Taiwan are a good example. Without exception, these students submit and receive their assignments with two hands, almost reverently. On top of that, when I pass any of them in the hall, they stop; give a short, polite bow; and say, "Good morning, Professor." Okay, admittedly, I like it—a lot. Who wouldn't? These students report that in their country, teachers are esteemed among the highest professionals. Respecting respectful students, from any family, country, or culture, is easy, and thankfully, there are many such students from all walks of life who bless our classrooms with their presence.

On the other hand, the characteristically difficult, disruptive, or disrespectful student poses a distinct challenge to the well-meaning intentions of an otherwise courteous teacher. A teacher at wit's end is understandably tempted, even provoked, to treat a difficult student in kind. A commitment to respect students and do no emotional harm requires patience and fortitude, especially in trying circumstances.

■ My physics teacher treated his students as human beings, not prisoners within his classroom. I didn't feel degraded, put down, unliked, or worthless—no one did. There was one troublemaker student in our class, hard to deal with and relate to. Our teacher was forced to send the student out of class and discipline him several times. Yet, in or out of class, I never saw our teacher treat that student any differently from another. He listened to the student, encouraged him, and supported him. No matter the conflicts that existed between them, our teacher refused to take it out personally on the student. In fact, one year this same student received the award for outstanding student in physics. This teacher gave credit where credit was due, regardless of the difficulties. (Heather)

Humanly speaking, teachers experience a flux of positive and negative feelings about students, like the ebb and flow of an ocean tide. But like an unpredictable current, feelings are unreliable for gauging appropriate responses to student misbehavior. Respect is a choice, an action, not a feeling. The commitment to respect students, even difficult ones, comes first, followed by the choice to interact with students in respectful ways. Then and only then can the heart follow in awakening feelings of positive regard.

According to founder and psychiatrist William Glasser (1998), quality schools are predicated on choice rather than coercion as a guiding philosophy. Relationships based on respect are a printed tenet of such schools. Glasser counsels teachers to be compassionate and courteous, avoiding put-downs and sarcasm no matter what students do. He cautions teachers to not respond to a profane and angry student in kind, an attitude that admittedly requires meticulous self-discipline but, in the long run, fosters more respectful student attitudes toward teachers.

Along this line of thinking, Lawrence-Lightfoot (2000) described an unusual incident involving a trusted and respected high school student who
came early to class one morning, walked up to the teacher's desk, and, completely out of character, pulled out a pocket knife and inexplicably waved it in
her face. Stunned but somehow resolute, the teacher fully faced the student,
and with inner fortitude she responded without anger, "That is illegal, put it
away now!" The student, troubled and broken by an incident outside of
school, faced consequences but never again disrespected the teacher and over
time returned to his customary trustworthy behavior.

There are, of course, no guarantees in the classroom. We speculate on
strategies that might have prevented the tragedies at Columbine and Virginia
Tech in a fog of despair and disbelief. The questions are many and the answers
few. Nevertheless, the case for choosing to respect each student from day one,
to cultivate a relationship regardless of natural feelings or inclination, and to
gather students in a safe cocoon lined with consideration foreshadows an opportunity to diffuse many difficult classroom situations.

■ She understood when we were having a bad day, and she showed us respect and understanding during our difficult times. You could count on
her, and many people respected her for that reason. (Veronica)

Students certainly do have bad days, many of them stemming from fallout
that occurs apart from the classroom, at times a spin-off from incidents at
home. Rhonda, my childhood playmate and a victim of parental disrespect, is
a good example. Not surprisingly, Rhonda had a notoriously short fuse. Nevertheless, I spent time with her regularly if not always harmoniously. One afternoon, when our interaction began to sour, Rhonda suddenly lurched at me,
taking a vampire bite from the base of my throat. Startled and horrified, I ran
home.

When my mother noticed blood trickling down my neck, she led me back
to Rhonda's house to resolve the issue. Standing on the front porch—two
sullen girls and their respective mothers—Rhonda's mother threatened her
with, "I'm going to knock your teeth out!" I knew she wouldn't, as I'd heard
that tone and talk from Rhonda's mother before. Still, this disrespectful encounter is indicative of the burden some students carry into the classroom. Indeed, for some students, a teacher might be the only adult who disarms them
with kindhearted respect and courtesy.

This is no easy task, to be sure. It takes vigilant persistence to remain authentically respectful, recognizing that placated respect is like a Halloween mask. Students can spot a phony anywhere. Exemplary teachers effuse respect like a natural mantra in all venues, from the classroom to the playground, to the teacher's lounge, and out to the hallways. It's who they really are inside. They are not just "acting" respectful; they are choosing to be respectful people.

TEACHER TALK

■ During my senior year in high school, I volunteered at a local elementary school, working with second and third graders every day for two hours. It amazed me how these teachers managed to make every student feel important. Even in the most trying of circumstances, they remained calm. There was a mutual feeling of love and respect between the teachers and students. I never once heard them speak badly about a student who misbehaved or who wasn't "getting" it. Instead they approached the situation in a new way and kept trying until they succeeded. These teachers had a huge impact on my life. I can only imagine the impact they had on the lives of their students. (Haley)

A commitment to talk and act respectfully is like a well-placed boomerang. Talk respect, and respect will circle back to the speaker. Called mutual respect, it is best experienced by a teacher when earned rather than commanded or coerced. It could be argued that coerced respect works better in a classroom than disrespect; nonetheless, respect based on fear is not deep, lasting, or heartfelt. More important, students do not translate coerced respect into respectful attitudes, attitudes that are an essential part of their education in human relations.

When I hear teachers commiserate with one another about students who do not respect teachers, I know that to be true in many classrooms. I've observed the palpable tension in classrooms and the frustration of hardworking teachers striving valiantly to help students learn. I have seen good teachers struggle to remain calm, only to "lose it" and regret it in the wake of the shattered remains of a student's self-respect. Blessedly, students are resilient. They notice and appreciate an apology, becoming more willing to reason and assume accountability for their part in building good relationships.

Teachers must work even harder in challenging classrooms to remember their ethical calling and consider ways to earn respect. Earned respect begins with teachers who model the classroom tone they deeply desire. Teachers who earn respect enjoy satisfying relationships with students that spill freely into improved student engagement and learning. Be assured that a commitment to building relationships is never at odds with a commitment to learning.

> ■ My high school teacher was personable; he treated students with respect and courtesy. Although he demanded a lot from us, the respect he earned allowed him to get a lot from his classes. (Kyle)

Respectful teachers grasp the magic of human relations, the longing of human souls, and the affirming power of attributed worth. Students differ so widely in disposition, capacity, and experience that their ways of approaching life in the classroom vary enormously. So fragile is human nature that we must preserve the worth of each individual student with awe and reverence.

Respect for student worth is not a static act; rather, it reaches out and draws students in, encircling them within the unbroken classroom community. In an encircled community, respect quenches a thirsty student's soul. A good teacher waters seeds of student worth daily while the tender plants grow strong and tall in the sunshine of unfettered acceptance. Such teachers embrace students and celebrate their variety, deeming variety as an opportunity to search deeply in the rich soil of student souls and, with wonder and expectation, cultivate new seedlings of untapped growth.

KEY IDEAS

✓ Teachers set the tone of classroom interaction, teacher to student, student to teacher, and student to student.

✓ Respect for students is a choice, independent of feelings.

✓ Respect is conveyed by words and actions and particularly by the tone underlying the words and actions.

✓ Listening carefully is the highest form of respect.

✓ True respect for students carries over to the teacher's lounge, where students cannot hear.

2

Encouragement

■ My band teacher solidified the idea that a teacher is not just someone who gives you information. He took the time to really know me, and over time he worked on different aspects of my life, characteristics that could be brought out. One time, when I was acting and dancing on stage, he said, "Joshua, if you could see yourself up there, you would realize that you could do anything." That one statement is what I remember if I don't feel the most confident or courageous. (Joshua)

THAT ONE STATEMENT

It would be difficult to quantify the number of words that teachers speak in any one day or any one school year, but certainly their words are many. Undoubtedly, teachers utter so many words that they can easily take the substance of those words for granted. Pieced together, words blend into statements, some routine and others honeycombed with significance. The potential power of a teacher's words, for good or ill, is not lost on students.

In the introduction to this book, I shared the story of Mrs. Houghton, my third-grade teacher, who took me aside following an oral report and said she believed I could be a good teacher. Mrs. Houghton went on about her business while I pondered her statement over and over in my young, pliable mind.

And therein lies how two perspectives—teacher and student—each attach significance to a particular statement. To Mrs. Houghton, her feedback formed just one of many kind statements she had shared with students over her long teaching career. To me, her encouraging words were life changing, remembered to this day, more than fifty years later. Because of the profound impact that a teacher's words can have on students to encourage or discourage, the substance of such interactions is worth exploring.

■ He was not only a teacher but someone to go to with a problem. I remember as a junior in high school, I received the results of my ACT, and it was lower than I and everyone else had expected. This teacher knew I was upset, and he said to me, "You know its hell to be thought of as average, but you're not average." And that statement meant so much to me. (Gabrielle)

A number of years ago, I craved encouraging words to ease the burden of my crushing load. Mired in the quicksand of graduate school, weary from simultaneously holding down a job while slogging through research, I began to sink beneath the strain of my overscheduled life. Although I deliberately set the course and pace of my journey through academic quicksand, it didn't stop me from whining at home and in the office.

My phlegmatic secretary allowed me a wide berth, enduring my grumbling with her characteristically gentle grace. One morning, sensing that I was stuck in a low point, my secretary threw me a lifeline. Focusing her attention toward me, she paused, smiled, and spoke low key, "If it was easy, everyone would do it." Taken aback, I quietly studied her words as she slipped away without further comment. Over time, her words continued to speak a powerful message: graduate school is hard, and you are pursuing a worthy goal that only the persistent few can endure. That one statement rearranged my outlook.

Make no mistake, life didn't get easier, but my secretary's words, spoken in passing, encouraged me to steadily plod through school and press forward toward completion. I pondered her message in the ensuing years and have since shared the same sentiment with my students who needed a lifeline. They react in the same way that I did: a startled smile, a moment of reflection, and a realization—aha—that I can do this too. Such is the power of encouraging words.

WRITTEN WORDS

■ As a sophomore I enrolled in speech and debate, not having much idea of what to expect. I was amazed not only by his knowledge but more by his dedication to individual students. After each of our speech tournaments, every member got an encouraging note, despite our victory or loss. It is amazing how one note can brighten a student's day. Never did a birthday or accomplishment go unnoticed. To this day, I have kept all the cards. Every now and then, I reread them for encouragement. I doubt that he will ever grasp to what extent he shaped my life and the lives around me. (Robert)

Encouraging words capture and mesmerize just as meaningfully in written notes as they do in verbal form, perhaps more so in their visible permanence. Like many teachers, I treasure a folder bulging with special notes students have written to me over the years. I wouldn't dream of discarding any one of them. From time to time, I poke around in that folder and indulge a few minutes to reread the thoughtful sentiments. I wonder why I don't write encouraging notes to my students more often.

Not long ago, my mother cleaned out her attic and stumbled on a dusty old stack of my elementary school report cards. Separating them one by one, I bandied about through these reports, which included a variety of grades, a smattering of work habit checks, and a chronology of my attendance. In the end, I focused less on the grades and checkmarks and more on my teachers' written comments that tagged me ready for promotion to the next grade.

As the teacher who particularly sparked my interest in teaching, Mrs. Houghton's words, penned and dated June 1956, caught my attention: "Sandra is a gentle, soft-spoken, and polite 'lady' who did very good work and contributed worthwhile things to our class." I had not seen this before. Interestingly, I also noticed that my attendance record was better that year than in any other year, indicative of a strong relationship with this teacher.

■ Of all the things that teachers have written, I remember her exact words in a note she wrote to me: "You don't always have to be perfect—it's okay to make mistakes." This made me feel like she was teaching for me and not at me. (Hannah)

Handwritten encouraging notes and comments are in danger of being aborted in our fast-paced lifestyle and replaced with lightning speed by a culture of e-mail and text messaging. Unmistakably, these "keep-in-touch" electronic systems serve us well. Nevertheless, modern communication modes and instant words can obscure the thoughtful, personal touch that handwriting affords. It doesn't take long; it may mean a lot.

STUDENT SELF-CONCEPT

■ She was an incredible woman who welcomed everyone with a smile. She broadened my horizons in drama and speech, and she strengthened my self-esteem, which is incredibly appropriate for adolescents going through puberty changes. I know that she cared about me and challenged me in an area in which I had never been challenged before. She helped me succeed when I didn't know I could be successful. (Courtney)

I read the account of a teacher who intended to encourage her students to identify and focus on the things they do well. In the midst of this self-reflective classroom activity, one of the students raised her hand and, responding for the whole class, challenged the teacher with a profound truth: "Most people tell us what we do wrong so how can we feel good about ourselves?" (Johnson and Johnson 1986).

Clearly, we want children to develop the personal insight to recognize their own unique capacities and not be dependent on the judgments of others. In spite of these ideals, a child's self-concept is created, to a greater extent than we might like to acknowledge, by adults. Indeed, a child's self-concept springs largely from the significant input of other people—first parents, reinforced later by teachers and peers. Conceptions of self burrow deep into a child's soul, holding fast like the tentacles of an octopus. Growing up, children often spend their lives living out the positive or negative consequences of the input they receive from others, including teachers.

■ She told us from day one that she gets the best students in her classes. Throughout the year she reminded us specifically about our abilities and said we were capable of so much. This led many students (myself included) to do our best in her class. I feel that she expressed this for a reason—so we would believe we were a good class and act accordingly—a self-fulfilling prophecy. (Natalie)

While the term *self-concept* refers to personal interpretations of one's overall worth, another term, *self-efficacy*, refers to personal interpretations that vary according to domain. Students, for example, have a distinct sense of self-efficacy for each of their academic subjects as they progress through school. A student may believe he is a capable reader but a poor speller. Likewise, a student may see herself as a talented athlete but rather unskilled in math.

Teachers have a part in shaping students' general self-concept as well as their self-efficacy for specific academic tasks, and insightful teachers stay alert for ways to genuinely encourage students' self-efficacy in areas where they believe students can excel. And it is important to recognize that all students can excel in some unique way.

Genuine encouragement, however, is fundamentally different from patronizing praise—a cheap imitation, like honey-coated flattery. An example of such patronizing praise is overusing the nonspecific phrase "good job," a counterproductive form of general flattery that increases student dependence on a teacher's continued praise (Kohn 1999).

Specific encouragement that focuses on a particular accomplishment, such as "the story you wrote has an intriguing plot," embodies supportive words that inspire academic self-efficacy for writing, and the specificity of the words encourages students to examine their own work, form their own interpretations, delight in their own accomplishments, and view mistakes as a way to make progress (Crabb and Allender 1984). Likewise, teachers, who readily admit their own mistakes encourage students to learn from experience while preserving their self-efficacy.

■ She was the adviser for our high school newspaper. We had just purchased two new Macintoshes, and no one knew how to use them. She encouraged us to play around with them and have fun using them. I remember one day when she accidentally trashed an entire folder of advertising layouts on the computer. She told us about it and didn't act like it was a big tragedy. She showed me that it was okay to make mistakes, okay to admit them and learn from them. (Crystal)

TOUGH SCHOOL YEARS

Many people can reflect back on their school days and point to one abysmal year. Reasons for a rough school year run the gamut from personal problems to monotony to lack of readiness, but whatever the contributing factors, the student came up short and needed encouragement to pick up and persevere. Teachers who have a knack for discerning shortfalls and student needs understand that well-placed, honest, and specific encouragement helps dissipate the accumulative impact of week after dreary week of rough patches in the classroom. For some students, such teachers helped them ease off the precipice of school failure and move in a decidedly new direction.

> ■ I owe a lot to her because she was the first teacher to get me interested in writing. We wrote poems and stories, and she encouraged my work; she noticed I was good at something, which encouraged me to do it more. Third grade was a rough year for me, but she was there to see me through my trials and tribulations. (Sarah)

Third grade was laden with trials and tribulations for my husband, Don, as well. He began first grade when he was just five, much too early for him to fully master reading, math, and spelling. Little was known about learning differences in the early 1950s when Don attended elementary school, and by the time he entered third grade, he struggled to swim his way out of the bottomless deep end of average performance.

Mrs. Bachelor, his discerning third-grade teacher, recognized Don's idle potential in several areas, and she sought to shore up his self-efficacy by teaching him new strategies for approaching schoolwork. In the meantime, Mrs. Bachelor let him know, both tacitly and explicitly, that grades were not the sum of a person; rather, she steadfastly maintained that character and attitude embodied what really mattered in the long haul.

Equally significant to Don, Mrs. Bachelor called him by his adult name—Don—rather than by his childhood nickname—Donnie, the first person to do so. The name change might seem inconsequential, something incidental to the real business of schooling, but it was not lost on a young boy who relished the soul nourishment that Mrs. Bachelor regularly supplied. This small lady with the big heart and happy disposition understood the magic of well-placed encouragement.

Rather than an overall rough school year, tough times may hover more specifically around a particular subject area, paralyzing a student with self-inflicted beliefs and labels, in effect echoing, "I'm not good at this," repeatedly in a student's mind. Good teachers refuse to let students indulge faulty beliefs and instead encourage them with useful thought patterns and renewed opportunities, as in the following two episodes.

■ Throughout my education, I have had trouble with math. However, with his patience, understanding, and good teaching techniques, my grades in math and all of my other classes improved that year. I had his class first hour, and sometimes I overslept. He made it possible to make up the tardiness or absences by coming into class an hour early. Whenever I took advantage of this opportunity, he helped me with my homework. He made math fun, and although my math courses during college are difficult and my grades are at a C average, I now enjoy the challenges. (Daisy)

■ I could count on my speech teacher to be there for me to give advice and just listen. One time I really flubbed up a speech. She gave me some encouraging words and suggested that I try again the next day. She was a very supportive teacher. (Chelsea)

ENCOURAGING THE DISCOURAGED

When it comes to encouraging the discouraged, Oscar the cat is an expert. Oscar lives in a Rhode Island nursing home and makes daily rounds to each wing of the advanced dementia unit. He employs his own brand of furry friendship and gentle care. Ignoring the more able patients, Oscar zeros in on those who most need his attention: those who don't have long to live.

With astounding accuracy, Oscar enters the room of a terminally ill resident, jumps up on the bed, examines his chosen patient, and curls up close to his new friend. Oscar remains, purring and nuzzling, until the patient passes. For many, nursing homes are uninviting places, populated by the weakest members of society, visited only by obligated family members, but Oscar dismisses the despair and, like a sentinel, stays close beside those he chooses to encourage. For his volunteer feline encouragement, the local hospice agency awarded Oscar a plaque citing his compassionate care (Dosa 2007).

We can learn something from Oscar about relationships. Everyone has burdens to bear, obstacles to overcome, and discouragements to endure. Students are not immune to life's difficulties. As with anyone, students, in the throes of discouragement, may wonder if anyone notices, cares, or understands. Such students are in every classroom, perhaps more numerous than we acknowledge.

Discouraged students may be physically in class but mentally and emotionally elsewhere. Certainly, difficult times and the painstaking process of working through the difficulties build character. A caring teacher may be instrumental in helping students make pivotal character building choices, particularly if the teacher withholds judgment and strives, instead, to encourage and assist.

■ High school is a hard time for students because there are so many self-esteem issues that come into play. When I was a sophomore, I had been suspended for the first four days of school. I was mortified. Mrs. K acknowledged my absence without scorn or judgment. She conferenced with me at various times and only displayed faith in my abilities. She often challenged me and rewarded my efforts with encouragement and my failures with support and advice. (Kim)

Late one semester, I engaged my teacher education students in a lengthy conversation about the essential need to encourage students as they work through difficulties, forge a self-concept, and build character. I well remember Jared's response. Jared, who planned to teach high school history, had listened closely in silence as the class wrestled with how teachers might encourage students more broadly, encompassing even students' personal lives when appropriate and necessary. Class members responded with the expected convictions, revealing the breadth of their commitment to support students as whole persons, not just as recipients of knowledge.

As the conversation continued, Jared, visibly discontented, finally raised his hand and patently stated his sentiment: "I just want to teach history; I don't want to deal with students' problems." His statement hung suspended over the class like a menacing cloud on an otherwise sunny day. Although Jared had already mastered teaching history, he had yet to master teaching students.

Beyond question, in the untidy realm of classrooms, there is little chance of isolating history or any other subject from students' lives outside the classroom. Along with their backpacks, students carry other burdens, at times more weighty than the books they bear. In the reality of growing up, problems will ever threaten student stability, plaguing them with discouragement, leaving them lost like the vulnerable Charlie Brown. Jared raised a valid point that most teachers are not professional counselors; however, sincerity and compassion go a long way toward bridging that gap with needed encouragement from a significant adult.

■ As a freshman, I was out sick because I had cancer. I am afraid to say that some of my teachers were not sure how to handle the situation. Some teachers said lots, and some didn't say anything. However, my English teacher was supportive without being overbearing. She told me not to worry about my assignments and gave me "modified" assignments that I could do at home. She called to see how I was doing, and she made a special attempt to "check up" on me. Now, although she is retired, she continues to "teach" me, and we are good friends. (Kelly)

In the normal cycle of classroom life, teachers expect that students will develop and thrive with optimum health and vigorous strength. After all, life's most devastating events belong to the old, not the young. And so, when life goes terribly wrong for any student, a teacher's attempts to shape appropriate and caring expressions may be overshadowed by an awkward sense of helplessness and a displaced understanding of a student's real needs.

I experienced that sense of helplessness and loss for just the right encouraging words when two of my students suddenly and unexpectedly faced the worst life can offer to those so young and healthy. One of my students, Cindy, a promising future mathematics teacher, received a frightful diagnosis: she had a brain tumor. It devastated her, her family, and her teachers, yet she valiantly maintained her optimistic outlook through a long and arduous recovery before returning to school.

Another student, Ron, a future elementary teacher and gifted athlete, succumbed to a freak skiing accident that left him paralyzed from the waist down. He, too, endured a lengthy recovery and months of therapy to help him prepare for life in a wheelchair. Through it all, Ron's enthusiasm for life never waned. Resilient students can teach us a great deal.

These two tragic incidents occurred in close sequence, and when Cindy and Ron returned to classes, I felt helpless, lost in a sea of hypothetical words and weak ideas to support their transition from rehabilitation back into teacher education. Quite simply, I decided that no mix of rehearsed elaborate words could change the situation. So, when all words seemed shallow and all gestures contrived, I chose simple expressions from my heart, encompassing my happiness to see them back in school and my desire to help them continue to plan for a bright future. They responded with gratitude and hard work.

Although unpredictable at the time, their future was indeed bright, as both Cindy and Ron are successful teachers today. Their persistence through pain foreshadowed the incredible professionals they were to become, their own lives a beacon of hope and encouragement for their students.

MISSED OPPORTUNITIES

In contrast to my satisfying connection with Cindy and Ron, I encountered a troubled student, Art, who had difficulty connecting with most everyone. Art attended eighth grade at a school where I chaired the school board. After a chain of reckless misdeeds, Art's teacher recommended to the principal that Art be expelled from school, and thus his case came before the board.

I still marvel how a simple, one-line agenda item can carry with it such potentially dire consequences. In the course of school board business and our lengthy discussion about Art's situation, I coveted Solomon's wisdom but had to settle for the assembled wisdom of the school board members, teachers, and administration.

At one point, Art appeared before the board, as did his parents. He wanted to finish eighth grade with the class he had been part of since kindergarten, but ultimately, in our collective and admittedly finite wisdom, the school board voted to ask Art and his parents to sever their connection with the school. It was an ugly time; Art's understandably angry parents sent me a series of irate letters with copies to other board members.

A year later, I happened to notice Art when I visited another school at which he had enrolled. He seemed settled enough, perhaps not thriving. I silently wished him the best but wondered from time to time how things might have been different—how the school personnel, the school board, and

I might have worked with him, taught him, and encouraged him. Might it have made a difference? I cannot know, but I wondered.

■ I was what teachers might say a very badly behaved student. I was on the honor roll every semester, but I was usually in some trouble. Then I came to be a student under Mrs. D. She saw that I really wasn't a bad kid; I was just bored. So she started letting me help tutor other students, grade papers, and just keep busy. She showed me that there are many children who just need individualized direction and extra motivation. (Mackenzie)

HOPE FOR THE FUTURE

Most teachers do not have the privilege of observing students morph from youngsters in the classroom to adults in society. The future advances quickly, assuredly, and we lose track of students as they change dramatically like butterflies emerging from cocoons. The difference that excellent teachers make in the classroom today, building relationships and encouraging growth, will populate the future with the striking evidence of a job well done.

■ My sixth-grade teacher taught more than just math, science, English, and history. He was an educator on life. He used every available opportunity to discuss personal skills and possible real-life situations that we, as students about to enter junior high, would use or be confronted with. He not only prepared us for algebra but also equipped us with the confidence and maturity to deal with new and upcoming changes by using illustrations and examples. Self-esteem, maturity, and determination were all stressed in his classroom. He discussed the real-life outcomes and consequences that evolved from being mature and working diligently. He not only made us feel like students but also acknowledged us as the hope for the future. (Christopher)

Thomas Jefferson, an early hope for America's future, studied law under George Wythe, the first American law professor in the young colonies. Wythe became Jefferson's mentor, acknowledging him as the hope of the future, molding his political philosophy, and encouraging Jefferson's potential greatness. As Jefferson struggled with writing the Declaration of Independence, he sent drafts to Wythe for review, and later Wythe added his signature to this historical document.

As his life drew to a close, Wythe left his considerable and valued library of law books to Jefferson, indicating that the books might not be worthy of a place in Jefferson's presidential museum but suggesting that the books were the most valuable possession he had to give—an incredible and humble symbol of encouragement from the teacher of an American president (Burstein 1995).

Encouraging and caring teachers understand the essential nature of their calling; they keep ever in mind that they are teaching students rather than content alone. Teaching students means more than seeing to it that students are diligently engaged in doing the business of school on any particular day— reading, writing, and arithmetic. Rather, such teachers offer whole-person care; they believe in students today and encourage possibilities for their future even in the absence of immediate evidence.

■ As a teacher, she was confident yet never proud or boastful. A boy in my class who was just waiting to be sixteen so he could drop out of school decided to finish out the last almost two years and graduate because of her. She never took credit for that. She gave the credit to him because even though she encouraged him to see that he could be successful, he was the one who made the decision. (Jade)

KEY IDEAS
✓ Encouraging words offered purposefully or in passing, verbally or in writing, imprint student lives more than we know, both now and in their future.
✓ Fumbling to form just the right words doesn't result in encouragement as much as sincerity and simplicity do.
✓ Keeping alert for opportunities to authentically encourage students may mean the difference between enabling failure and charting success.

3

The Gift of Time

■ He conquered the 8 A.M. to 3 P.M. teacher syndrome. It was standard for him to arrive early and leave late. From my first course as a freshman in high school, I could see a fire in him to teach. Later, upon entering college, I had to take a placement test. For three hot summer nights, four or five hours a night, he traveled the fifteen-mile distance to the school just to teach me! Remarkably, everything I learned through high school resurfaced in those three nights, and I easily passed the proficiency test. (Alex)

THE TROUBLE WITH TIME

The trouble with time is that we don't have enough of it. Lack of time is a universal complaint, and teachers are no different from other people who juggle multiple priorities in a 24/7 life. No doubt, in a contest of demanding schedules, teachers will claim a berth among the winners. If challenged, teachers, with some justification, will argue that the general public cannot really fathom an educator's life.

When I taught in high school, people envied my profession: "8 A.M. to 3 P.M. with summers off," they would say wistfully. That simplistic characterization of a teacher's life falls with a thud on those who live it day in and day out. In truth, teachers are not just teachers from 8 A.M. to 3 P.M. The teaching profession is all-consuming and at times overwhelming, flooding into every niche of a teacher's life. To be sure, most of a teacher's work takes place outside the classroom, apart from the 8 A.M. to 3 P.M. formal shift.

When teachers are not grading papers, attending meetings, preparing lessons, or organizing learning materials, their thoughts regularly and decidedly pull back to the classroom like the receding ocean tide. They reflect on the day's events, consider Johnny's indifference, or grapple with Suzy's academic struggles. They consider new and better ways to teach a certain concept or strengthen their relationship with a particular student.

A good teacher is a teacher all the time, not just in front of students. In the face of such time demands, exemplary teachers somehow stretch the confines of their job description to collect students beyond 8 A.M. to 3 P.M., those hungry to understand, and those too shackled with misconceptions to care. Such teachers gather their students before school, after school, anytime, in purposeful attempts to build mentoring relationships and help students bridge the gap between what they already know and what they need to understand.

■ I knew I wasn't good at chemistry, so I never tried. I gave up hope of passing that subject. Then a new teacher took over the class! At first he seemed demanding, and all of my classmates started complaining, but he didn't give up, especially on people like me. Before an exam he would call some of us to come to his office after school. We really didn't appreciate his help at first. But later he even waited for us until 6 P.M. when we had other activities. This really changed me. He gave me a reason to study—after all, there's nothing that we cannot achieve (if only we try!), and I passed with distinction! (Summer)

Many amazing teachers willingly dedicate whatever time is necessary beyond the classroom confines to reteach or clarify content. Their commitment is admirable, in part because standing in classes all day, working with 30 to 130 different students, presenting, explaining, facilitating, transitioning, or summarizing, is demanding and draining work.

I often return home from a day of teaching and shut down for a while, wanting nothing more than superficial contact with others. With this in mind, the teachers who spend some of their precious time outside regular classroom hours to assist and mentor students deserve a medal of honor. In reality, whatever it takes to help students learn is the substance of a teacher's task, after school, before school, and, for some teachers, even on weekends. When teachers embrace the task with unselfish devotion, students, like those who follow, remember years later.

■ My most memorable experience with her was in our advanced place-ment American history class. We not only met in school; she also gathered us for an hour on Sunday afternoons. She gave us her all and we wanted to do the same. (Isabelle)

■ He was a student-oriented teacher. Each class began with him asking, "Are there any questions?" He wanted questions during his lectures, and he would stall his lecture as long as possible to answer each one. After class he was flogged with students, but he made time for us all. (Steven)

■ He gave anything he did 110 percent! He stayed late to help our group even after he had been at school for ten hours! (Autumn)

EXTRA ACADEMIC TIME

The striking range of diverse students, each with differing areas of strength, weakness, and interest, resembles an academic teeter-totter with student mo-tivation and achievement alternating from high to low for each student at one time or another. These unpredictable highs and lows ignite the most re-sourceful teachers to dismantle the typically prescribed curriculum—and their more ordinary instructional strategies—to devote a great deal of addi-tional time and concentrated effort to figuring out ways to lift students who remain stuck on the low end of the teeter-totter.

■ I had a lot of problems with reading. My second-grade teacher helped me overcome my fears. She was concerned that I had some kind of learning disability, and she set up several tests to hopefully eliminate any psychological or physiological problems. Once they de-termined there were no problems, she used several teaching methods and interpersonal skills to help me. First and foremost, she spent a great deal of extra time with me. She did this in a way that I would not feel excluded from the rest of the class. For example, when we were put into groups, she made it seem like she picked the groups randomly, when in reality we were grouped with children of similar ability. (Madison)

When it comes to schooling proficiency, there are scores of students who struggle through the unknown, like wandering a bewildering labyrinth, getting lost at times until a teacher steps in to carefully guide their way spending considerable time as comrades in the journey. This is particularly true for students who meander a maze of unknown content while simultaneously wrestling to learn English.

I encountered such a learning labyrinth during an accreditation visit to an elementary, middle, and high school located on the same campus. Small in size and student population, the school conveyed a reputation for individual time and attention that attracted international students from Korea and other Asian countries. Although these students took diagnostic tests at the beginning of the school year, the teachers had an insufficient understanding about how to guide this guest student population through the maze of language barriers.

As I visited from classroom to classroom, I noticed that many of the international students sat politely but remained inert and tuned out like a group of subway commuters with veiled eyes. Our accreditation team followed up and worked with the administration and teachers as a plan for both teacher development and student progress evolved and took form, a plan that required an extended time commitment, varied methods, and individual instruction. In the long run, the school enhanced its overall effectiveness and salvaged its reputation for individual student attention by devoting the necessary time to address the needs of the diverse population it chose to enroll.

TIME FOR DIFFERENTIATION

■ I have always had trouble with math in school, but she helped me to get an "A" in geometry. She never got frustrated with our class even though it was a basic level class and we didn't always understand the concepts. She sat down with us individually and worked with us at our own pace using different methods until we understood what we were doing. This extra time and attention is essential in any classroom of students with special needs. She related to us and made us laugh, which is important—especially in a class as stressful as math. I don't think I will ever forget her. (Chloe)

All students can learn but not always at the same pace or in the same cookie-cutter way. Inventive teachers extend their limited instructional time by differentiating approaches to content and activities. In so doing, they efficiently reach a wider spectrum of students while fostering successful learning experiences and building mentoring relationships. We explore learning activities more extensively in chapter 7. For purposes here, I advance the idea that differentiating instruction eventually saves time for busy teachers.

Differentiation involves organizing instruction in unique and varied ways to meet the needs of diverse students (Tomlinson 2001). Although it requires additional planning time, differentiating instruction actually saves time in the long run from the remediation required when students abort learning because of strategies that confuse, constrain, or hurry them. Unlike simply giving some students more assignments and some students less, differentiation entails adapting the nature of schoolwork.

Of course, teachers cannot realistically orchestrate all manner of lessons for each of the 30 to 130 or more students, nor do they have adequate time to individually tutor each student. And so, by differentiating instruction with a reasonable repertoire of approaches, teachers find that content and processes fit most students' needs much of the time. There are three basic ways to differentiate instruction:

✓ Differentiate the content—As a warm up, preassess students' understanding of a concept. Some students can move ahead, and some will need more direct instruction.

✓ Differentiate the process—Incorporate a variety of ways to learn content by engaging students in drawing, acting, discussing, writing, speaking, and singing.

✓ Differentiate the product—Offer choices for demonstrating learning, such as an oral description, labeled diagram, picture, collage, clay sculpture, debate, demonstration, interview, photo essay, mobile, musical play, time line, term paper, portfolio, or display.

The purpose of differentiating instruction is to help students warm up to the content and stretch various mental capacities much like athletes stretch various muscles to improve performance. When used regularly, differentiation can save remediation time by varying approaches to better engage a wider spectrum of students.

TUTORING TIME

■ School was never easy for me, and I would get pretty frustrated at times. My teacher was always, always available. He took any amount of time I needed outside of class to tutor me, and he never made me feel like a pain. He is one of the main reasons I had enough courage to go on to college. (Whitney)

Most teachers would like to tutor those students who need extra help; they recognize that such individual time builds strong relationships, but they have limited time for adequately addressing student needs alone. Teachers need all the help they can get to add instructional hours to their hectic day, and enlisting knowledgeable parents, grandparents, and volunteers offers an academic lifeline to students and a time-saving gift for teachers. Several years ago, I offered to help a teacher by participating in a pullout tutoring program for English-language learners at an elementary school. It was time well spent.

I tutored Taye, a seventh grader who, with his parents, immigrated to the United States from Ethiopia for better educational and economic opportunities. Taye's supportive parents had two basic goals for him. They wanted him to improve his English and comprehend his textbook readings.

I first saw Taye when he hesitantly approached a corner table in the school library where we met three days a week. Taller than the other seventh graders, he presented a stoic demeanor that masked his rather limp handshake. He remained quiet at first, and I concluded that he didn't want to be here, in the library with me, singled out from his classmates for tutoring—a typical and tenuous beginning for our sessions. It took several awkward meetings before Taye met my eyes fully, with his shy but expressive glance.

His greatest academic challenge was reading comprehension, due mainly to his inability to sound out words, so our sessions generally began with a phonics card game. Within a few days, he got the hang of the game, which didn't rely solely on pronunciation, and, more often than not, he thoroughly trounced me.

Trust came slowly, but with incremental success in the phonics game and his improving English, we gradually forged a good tutor–tutee relationship. We progressed steadily from rudimentary exercises in sounding out words to dynamic readings of *Hardy Boys* mysteries, daring each other with who could be most expressive. Taye found it less fun to pore over his writing or dig into his textbooks, but pore and dig we did, racking up hours that his teacher did not have in a classroom of twenty-five other students.

One day, Taye appeared in the library armed with his American history text. With an audible groan, he opened the book to a chapter that highlighted the Civil War. I regarded him and mused that Taye, recently transplanted from Ethiopia, would have no prior knowledge about the American Civil War. We needed some basic visual aids to lighten the mood and lift his grim expression.

Together, we drew an amateur but acceptable map of the United States, and I asked Taye to pinpoint where he lived in California. Referring to the right side of the map, I pointed out the eastern and southeastern states predominantly involved in this war. We followed with a time line rendering, on large poster paper, that spanned 1860 to the present time, and we marked off critical events in U.S. history; some of these he knew, but most he did not. The map and time line gave perspective to the succession of real-life, grueling, and inspiring war stories we read and discussed.

Without tutoring, I could only imagine Taye's frustration, slogging through Civil War history with his American classmates, who could retrieve the mental map and time line that Taye and I steadfastly built together. Pressed for time, his teacher might have skipped or hurried through this critical link to Taye's understanding.

With tutoring, Taye posed questions that he might otherwise have left unasked. In this, my first tutoring experience, I learned the inestimable value of individual guidance and the reward of service. While a student can tune out and mindlessly wither in a classroom filled with students, it is impossible to remain invisible during one-on-one time. Not every student has the tutoring opportunity that Taye had, but if needed and recruited, tutoring time offers a catalyst of hope and opportunities for bulding mentoring relationships.

INFORMAL ACADEMIC TIME

■ In high school, I was interested in literature and English. Sometimes, though, I felt rather alone because many of my friends were more interested in other subjects. My high school English teacher made me realize that it was okay to be different. She took extra time to read my writing and even encouraged me to enter several contests. When I won, she almost always went with me to the award ceremonies, even if it meant she had to drive me there and miss a day of school. (Grace)

Teachers who extend their heavy schedule to spark student curiosity and intellectual growth outside regular class time deserve special notice. For example, our daughter, Karen, had a dedicated teacher who determined that one of Karen's term papers held promise and possibility for an arena beyond school walls. He worked tirelessly to build their mentoring relationship and to help her polish her work and make it suitable for a presentation among professionals at a regional conference. Karen will not soon forget his time commitment to quality education.

Discerning teachers who take the time to encourage what their students accomplish outside the regular classroom find it enlightening to see students from a new perspective. Students are fascinating people; they have a host of experiences that embody their lives outside the 8 A.M. to 3 P.M. time that they spend sequestered in classrooms. Students have received awards, traveled, tinkered with hobbies, participated in community activities, come from interesting families, and lived in interesting places.

Several years ago, one of my students dazzled and enlightened me with his beyond-the-classroom accomplishments. I had not particularly connected with Nick, a gregarious student, almost larger than life, with a satirical personality and bellowing laugh. In class, he regularly annoyed me with his biting humor and glib bravado. Because of our rather tepid relationship, I was surprised when he invited me to attend his community presentation. Nick had spent a year teaching in Japan and was scheduled to discuss his experiences at a church gathering. I agreed to attend but had no idea what to expect.

When I arrived at the event a bit early, I noticed Nick onstage, dressed in the traditional Japanese kimono and Geta sandals, and I observed him focus carefully on his set up for a multimedia presentation. His apparent preparation impressed me, and I was hard pressed to dismiss the guilty feelings that recurred in my thoughts like a pesky fly. In truth, I had short-circuited the time to get to know Nick just because he had generally rankled me in class. Now, as I glanced around at the audience, I surmised that one other lady and I were the only teachers who attended his presentation, here to see Nick from a new perspective.

As the program commenced, Nick nodded my way, acknowledging my presence. He finessed his way through a marvelous travelogue punctuated with his satirical humor and infectious laugh, and it jarred me to fully recognize that all students have interests and experiences that teachers know nothing about. I further recognized that Nick's compendium of experiences and photographs—the customs he encountered and the teaching he lived—would prove useful to our class discussions.

Attending Nick's presentation powerfully transformed our relationship in the classroom. Instead of being annoyed at his satire, I dove in with him, and we enjoyed a friendly, dry, back-and-forth banter for our remaining years as teacher and student. We grew to appreciate what each other had to offer, and throughout our time in class, his experiences in Japan sprouted here and there like spring tulips to colorfully illustrate and enrich learning for all my students. Undoubtedly, Nick and his wealth of world experience could have lain dormant, invisible, if I had not bothered to find out who he was in more informal settings.

After Nick graduated, I didn't see him for more than two years, but he recently e-mailed me for some advice, and the contact reminded me that the extra effort in spending time with students, focusing on their interests, and sharing new interests with them nurtures a mentoring relationship that continues long after 8 A.M. to 3 P.M.

■ She talked the administration into allowing her to add to her already large teaching load by offering two semesters in environmental studies. She taught students respect and consideration for the land. She shared her thoughts, her experiences, and her resources. She shared her home, her time, and companionship outside the classroom when she took us all over northern New Mexico to study ecosystems, communities, and how they are intertwined. (Jocelyn)

QUALITY TIME WITH STUDENTS

The desire for time and attention is universal. Consider our cat Darby, for instance. Darby likes my husband better than he likes me. Darby's preference for Don doesn't really make sense, at least not to me. After all, we adopted Darby because I wanted him, and I'm the one who tends to all his needs. I feed him, I give him fresh water, I brush his long Himalayan coat, I even clean his litter box. Why shouldn't he like me best? Nevertheless, my fluffy white cat is most content when he curls up on Don's lap for hours, like an unmelted snowball.

The routine is familiar. Don and I arrive home from work, and Darby meows incessantly, waiting impatiently at ankle level, planted firmly between

Don's feet and mine. Darby's attention-hungry presence precludes us from a few precious minutes to review our day. Unfazed by our efforts to sidestep him, Darby continues a pathetic meow until Don scoops him up and settles into a big, comfy armchair for a proper greeting. Darby purrs loud enough to start an old engine as he nuzzles contentedly into Don's lap, resting his small head and front paws on Don's chest. And so Don spends quality time with Darby, talking to him like a buddy at a ball game, convincing Darby of his prized feline status in our family.

At times, I playfully interrupt this relationship, coaxing Darby to change to my lap with a plaintive "Darby, are you playing favorites?" Without skipping a purr, Darby lethargically turns in my direction, yawns widely, and stares at me for a moment before wrapping his tail around his feet and head, burrowing once again deep into Don's lap. To be sure, Darby will occasionally switch and curl awkwardly on my lap, appeasing me so I will feed him, brush him, and keep his litter box clean, but his usual choice is the one who gives the quality time and attention he desires. In short, Darby cares less about the maintenance tasks I perform and more about the pure time Don gives him.

Children crave quality time and attention too. From the time they are old enough to realize that people watch what they do, that their parents or others admire, laugh, and revel in their childish and fun-loving ways, children learn to covet an adult's valuable and limited time.

This reality played out on a recent visit when our young grandson, Jack, curiously watched me apply my makeup. He pressed me to finish, appealing for us to read books and build block cities. I stalled him for a bit, and he disappeared, but his eagerness for us to spend time together increased with each return to my vanity table. Finally, I asked Jack if he wanted a beautiful grandmother, complete with fresh makeup, or an ugly grandmother like the witch in *Snow White*. He replied, "I want an ugly grandmother who plays with me."

Make no mistake, the need for time and attention does not diminish when children attend school. I've not yet met a student, of any age or grade level, who fails to appreciate quality time and attention. It's so obvious and basic to good teacher–student relationships. And speaking of time and attention, I must confess to an astounding coincidence.

Administrators at the university where I teach invited faculty members to a party one night to welcome and spend time with the incoming freshmen. Absurdly busy, I needed to race home and finish writing this chapter on "spending time" with students. How could I possibly attend this event? As I packed my briefcase, I experienced a wave of uneasiness followed by dubious laughter at my hypocrisy. I went to the event, shook 400 freshmen hands, and enjoyed the time spent with these students. Later, I arrived home more focused on the message of this chapter rather than the pretense of its words.

■ She did a lot of stuff outside of school with us, like going to baseball games, going to the Little Dipper ice cream shop, going to the park, going to her house for dinner. I look back and am amazed at how much time she put into her students outside of the classroom. And it wasn't like she did this for just a few of her favorite students. She didn't deprive anyone; everyone got to go somewhere. She went, as they say, way above and beyond the call of duty. (Michael)

■ He had pool parties twice a semester at his house for all the students to come over and have fun. He made us a part of his life. He ate lunch with us—not always in the teachers' lounge. He stuck around after school for any student who wanted to talk, and he had the best sense of humor. (Vicky)

Most teachers I know need a break to replenish their energy. Recharging teacher batteries is essential, and teachers clearly have more to give when their cup is full. Once in a while, however, casual time with students over lunch or in other venues can unexpectedly energize teachers, not artificially like the Energizer bunny but authentically with a satisfied heart that binds with student hearts and absorbs their joy.

Ron Clark (2004a, 2004b), the teacher I described in an earlier chapter, is a good example. This "southern boy" chose to leave North Carolina behind and embrace a school in Harlem with his burning passion to help struggling students. Overestimating the possibility of his positive impact, this stranger, transplanted from the rural South to the urban North, choked in his early attempts to ally with his students.

Undeterred, he chose to hang around and be available to join students in their free-time activities. Jumping rope, a favorite student pastime, proved a good place to start. Instead of retreating to the teacher's lounge for all of lunchtime, Clark ventured outside with his students to observe and practice double-Dutch jump rope.

After three months of unsuccessful but steadfast attempts, Clark nearly abandoned the playground for the teacher's lounge, except for his students who came to appreciate how Clark made spending time with them a charming habit rather than an onus obligation. The students warmed to him, talking him through the convoluted Double-dutch technique, teaching him step-by-step until he mastered it, and won the hearts and minds of his streetwise students.

■ Our teacher always came to watch sporting events (I played volleyball and soccer). He sat around and joked with us before and after games. I knew if I ever needed him, he was there. (Paige)

PRECIOUS RESOURCE

Teachers are not rich. The one gift teachers can give is their time, and it has no price tag. Teachers teach from 8 A.M. to 3 P.M., but it is not the only time they teach. Be assured, teachers teach all the time in the way they live, the way they instruct, and the way they choose to spend time connecting with students. Teachers teach not only in the classroom but also in social gatherings, sporting events, the lunchroom, field trips, after-school mentoring, and before-school conversations.

Education, after all, is not an event from 8 A.M. to 3 P.M. It is eminently a verb rather than a noun, a calling that offers the gift of time over and over. Teachers whom students remember are those who choose to be authentically in the present with students whether in or out of the classroom. And thus, education encompasses what we pass on formally and informally. Education is a series of actions embodied in the most precious resource teachers have to give—their time.

KEY IDEAS

✓ Tapping a few minutes here and there to give students quality individual time and attention goes a long way in meeting their fundamental human needs.

✓ Mentoring, tutoring, and differentiation take time, but they build relationships and save time in the long run.

✓ Students have fascinating outside interests that will transfer effectively to the classroom when teachers take the time to discover student interests and celebrate their accomplishments.

4

Teacher–Student Friendships

■ The main characteristic that I especially liked about her was her friendly attitude. We learned while we had fun. We talked with her if we had a problem, and she helped us out whenever possible. When she moved to a different school, I felt like I lost a best friend. (Ryan)

DIFFERENT WORLDS

Charlotte and Wilbur, a spider and a pig, existed worlds apart. They could not have been more different, yet the two forged a close, mentoring friendship in the classic tale *Charlotte's Web* (White 2002). Spinning a web of hope and courage in good times and bad, the mature Charlotte systematically mentored the naive Wilbur, teaching him life lessons that ministered to Wilbur's downcast spirit and giving him the courage to believe in himself.

Although Wilbur did not win the pig-category blue ribbon at the county fair, he mastered lessons that shaped his character to a far greater extent than what could be offered through visible rewards and tangible accolades. In the end, Wilbur's eternal optimism reciprocated to his mentor, and Wilbur became Charlotte's support when she most needed it.

Like Charlotte and Wilbur, teachers and students exist in different worlds, and like Charlotte, one of the challenges teachers face is figuring out appropriate ways to bridge the gap between the two worlds. Students characterize teachers who connect the two worlds successfully with a term that seems suitable to them—*friend*—but steering the delicate balance and boundaries within teacher–student friendships requires great care and considerable insight.

■ She was fair and open minded. She was a friend when you needed her to be, but she knew where to draw the line. (Andrea)

BALANCE AND BOUNDARIES

To be honest, teacher educators get nervous when students describe one of their past teachers as a friend, particularly when these same students disclose their intent to be "friends" with their own students someday. The fear is that teachers, in their wish to be popular with students, will blur the boundaries between their responsibility as a teacher and their quest to be a friend.

In navigating the complexities of building strong relationships, teachers who prioritize friendship above other considerations are in danger of fooling themselves and confusing their students about the nature of teacher–student relationships. In a confused relationship, a teacher's sacred trust to guide intellectual development and assess student performance is easily and often irreparably compromised.

Ethical questions about the nature of teacher–student relationships are decidedly unique and different as students progress from elementary to middle school to high school and on to college. Although no grade level is immune, high school and college are especially vulnerable times when students can become embroiled in an emotionally dependent relationship and teachers can overstep appropriate boundaries.

Educators remain guarded and cautious about the extent to which teachers and students can or should be friends. Ideally, teachers and students coexist within a trust-based relationship, one in which teachers nurture students but steadfastly foster their independence (Plaut 1993). Wise teachers understand this, and they distinguish the appropriate line while fostering warm and friendly relationships with all students.

■ He was memorable from the very first day. He walked briskly into class, came up to the podium, and proceeded to lecture on the rules of the classroom. His voice boomed throughout the room and I'm sure down the hallway. He kept this up for the first week and then became an old softy. I know the reason he did this was to command re-spect. After he had accomplished that, he became our friend. (Laura)

In their inexperience, new teachers are the most vulnerable to misplaced friendship with their students. For example, late one spring, I received word that a local high school had hired Susan to teach full time for the coming school year. Susan, one of my brightest seniors, had completed all the re-quirements for a teaching credential except student teaching.

In my mind, student teaching is a nonnegotiable requirement, essential for real-world preparation in the nitty-gritty of classroom life. On the other hand, Susan, an indebted college student, saw no reason to turn down a lucrative job offer. She basked in the affirmation that accompanied this opportunity, and she planned to complete student teaching requirements simultaneously with her first year of teaching. I was assigned to observe, mentor, and evaluate her progress—and I was concerned.

Susan's appearance and demeanor, young and attractive, more like a high school senior than a college senior, red-flagged my apprehension. Reticent, al-most Bambi-like, Susan lacked the experience or natural assertive nature to supervise high school students. I suggested that she spend sufficient time in the summer reflecting on her approach to students and developing a class-room management plan. She later admitted to spending most of her summer assembling resources and planning lessons, a worthy but insufficient endeavor for the complex demands that lie ahead.

Apparently, Susan wanted to connect with her students right away, and she did so by engaging curious students' questions about her personal life, taking pictures arm in arm with students, and inviting students to her office for lunch. She meant well, of course, and many students became her friend, but these casual relationships had a predictable and devastating impact in her classroom. Students simply did not take her seriously as a teacher.

The days I observed in Susan's classroom revealed a series of management disasters that left me feeling uncomfortable and frustrated. On one such day, students freely conversed among themselves as class began, ignoring Susan's pleas for decorum and attention to the tasks at hand. Students walked in and out of the classroom at will. One student left and later returned with a box of cereal, a carton of milk, and a bowl, proceeding to crunch through her break-fast, unmindful of the disturbance it caused.

Several students opened the side windows and sat on the windowsills, suspended precariously and calling out to students below. Other students made rude, inappropriate comments, daring Susan to kick them out of class. Susan struggled to maintain her authority and composure, and students later characterized her as Bambi in a rage.

To her credit, Susan worked diligently to regain boundaries as the year wore on endlessly, and she implemented a number of interesting projects amid the chaos, but ultimately she did not return to the same high school the following year. She took time off to reenergize and to pursue other interests. When Susan later returned to teaching, she had a clear plan, and her classroom looked and felt entirely different. No longer did she prioritize making friends above establishing an effective learning climate. And, by establishing appropriate boundaries first, she became both an effective teacher and a friend.

■ Many of my high school teachers were either so friendly with their students that they lost control and respect of the class or so strict that they were seen as virtual monsters! Mr. H retained the delicate balance between authority and friend. I went to him several times as a personal counselor, and he treated me as a person whom he liked and respected, but he never lost his authority. He was not afraid to be the teacher, secure in his position and confident. I respect that attitude immensely. (Heather)

Teacher–student relationships are unique, complex, and delicate. In the realm of appropriate relationships, conventional wisdom ordains that students and teachers are not destined for friendship given the ominous risk of boundary confusion. What then do students mean when they sincerely respect a particular teacher, when the boundaries are appropriate, and when students still characterize the teacher as a friend? To what extent and in what way can teachers and students be friends?

A genuine teacher–student friendship develops slowly within the context of carefully established boundaries and mutual respect. In this context, a teacher friend is fundamentally different from the familiar, casual term *friend*. Indeed, a teacher friend is not someone to hang out with at the local mall, someone to date, or someone obliged by a parental role. What then are teacher friends, according to students who know and admire them? How does teacher friendship shine clearly through multiple facets of classroom life, like a carefully cut diamond?

VALUING STUDENTS

In one essential facet of classroom life, a teacher friend relates to students in a way that convinces each student of his or her inestimable value, like a priceless gift, packaged with matchless talents needed by the whole class—so much so, that the class would not be the same without a particular student's presence. Such value-laden eminence sooner or later kindles student speculation, "Could it be that I am this teacher's favorite?"

■ When I think back to her, I recall that I was one of her favorites, or at least that's what I thought at the time. Now I know she probably made everyone feel that way. (Lauren)

Our daughter, Karen, loved her second-grade teacher, Mrs. Anderson, whose inner attitude of joy oozed from every pore. She clearly valued each child in her classroom—a relaxed, confident person who enjoyed teaching—and especially delighted in the primary age-group to which she gravitated. Karen and our son, Kevin, fancied themselves as Mrs. Anderson's favorites, basking securely in her smile and tender disposition, their childhood antics a source of her delight rather than her consternation.

One time, my husband and I needed to be out of town, and Mrs. Anderson, whose daughter and son were away at college, offered to let Karen and Kevin stay with her in her home for the weekend. Ecstatic, our children carefully packed their overnight bags to visit Mrs. Anderson and her equally kind-hearted husband. Like favored children, Karen and Kevin pretended to be Mrs. Anderson's own offspring for the weekend, savoring the moments when she inadvertently called them Terry and Tom, after her own grown children.

For a couple of days, Karen and Kevin cherished what they believed to be an expression of favoritism from a favored teacher. True to her calling, Mrs. Anderson embraced many such temporary children, loving them all equally; each and every child held a favorite distinction in this teacher's heart, and each one knew it.

■ From what I recall, she didn't play favorites, she allowed all of us to succeed, and by not showing favoritism, she let each child feel special. Of all the teachers I had, she was the only one who attended my wedding. I hope I will be a teacher like her. (Kate)

NAMES AND FACES

One important way to feed friendly relationships is to refer to students by name. Quite naturally, students feel special when teachers not only know them as current students but also remember them long after they move on to new classrooms. Considering the scores of students that teachers see over the years, sorting out a knotty clump of previous students to distinguish each one by name is difficult at best. I suspect that most teachers try admirably but remain marginally successful. Likewise, it's no less bewildering to master student names in the first place.

A middle school teacher shared her struggle to sort student faces and attach them to 103 names over the first month of school. With single-minded focus, she worked at connecting names with faces and generally succeeded with most students. Two of her sixth-grade boys, however, presented an elusive challenge. Although unrelated, Matt and Mike both had blond hair and round cherub faces. With nearly identical names and similar in size, Matt and Mike delighted in fooling this teacher with their twinlike appearance and demeanor.

Fortunately, Matt had one distinguishing feature that separated him decidedly from Mike—a Mohawk-type hairstyle—and in the end, that's how the teacher came to remember and refer to them by name. All went well in the name game, until one day Matt and Mike both came to class with huge grins and identical Mohawk hair styles. Their explicit plan to mix up their teacher worked for a time, and I'm told that they keep trying new identity tricks for fun. Games aside, all students hope to be personally known and remembered by their teacher.

■ This young teacher related well to students, almost like a big sister. Every day she had a smile on her face, but the students also respected her because she kept the class in line. I still see this teacher every once in a while, and she asks how school and my activities are going. It always makes me feel good when a teacher remembers my name and my person. (Ann)

Although I consider myself organized in every way, student names are my downfall, off-balancing me like a tumbling Jill. I envy teachers who can retrieve names as quickly as Internet bookmarks. Blessedly, I once taught at a small college whose registrar affixed a picture beside each name on a class roster. What a satisfying coup—approaching each new class confidently to readily recognize each student. Even without pictures, I'm adept at memorizing student names within the first couple of days, and I blithely retain them as long as students stay in my class.

On the other hand, my anxiety builds when I encounter students years later in another setting. I remember their faces, their demeanor, even their work, but more often than not, I've forgotten their names. Searching, my memory taunts me like early dementia. I'm tempted to haplessly lay out a vaguely familiar name that resides in my neural cobwebs but hesitate to humiliate myself and the student.

Knowing that students appreciate the courtesy of a remembered name, I determined to improve or at least avoid tumbling down the entire hill. Lately, when I've forgotten a name, I still greet the person with a smile born of genuine happiness to see my former student, and I simply ask the student to "remind me of your name." It works. No student has ever been put off by this honest interaction. Once the "name thing" is put to rest, students seem pleased that I'm not fumbling awkwardly for the right name and the right words to engage them in conversation. Hopefully, they still see themselves nestled among my many student friends.

HONEST GIVE-AND-TAKE

■ This teacher was honest enough to tell us the truth. Most importantly, he let us make mistakes. He advised us if something might not work but allowed us to try if we felt like we had to. To top this off, he had a great sense of humor and spent time just talking to us about life in general while we worked on assignments. It helped us look beyond the teacher exterior, and he became human to us, a friend, definitely not an enemy. (Olivia)

All people, children or adults, need someone to talk with honestly and openly, someone approachable, someone who will listen. Honesty is a prerequisite for mentoring friendships. Ayers (2001) points out that an honest relationship between teachers and their students entails the kind of solidarity in which compassion and criticism, acceptance and advice, and celebration and guidance are equally the substance and bedrock of give-and-take in conversing and listening.

Such a relationship may have bumps in the journey, but authenticity breeds both security and freedom, and the journey fosters a relationship in which both teachers and students grow. Over time, students prefer authentic interactions with approachable teachers to interactions that are sugarcoated but transparently phony.

■ He listened to me when I came to him and didn't understand directions. He often explained it another time just for me. Once, I worked on a summation paper of ten pages, and my computer crashed, and I lost the whole thing. Again, he worked with me. He knew me and knew I loved the topic and worked hard and simply did not bullshit him to get out of work. I gained a friend as well as a mentor in that class. (Tom)

Approachable teachers occupy an enormous space in the lives of students, and they are well positioned to listen if they underscore the opportunity with honesty, sincerity, and interest. Fortunately, I had that approachable kind of teacher during my roller-coaster senior year in high school when, only two weeks before graduation, my steady boyfriend of the past year broke up with me in favor of another girl. Naturally, high school puppy-love romances come and go, but still, I felt brokenhearted and clueless.

As for my friends, acquaintances, and teachers, nothing could escape the grapevine buzz in the small high school I attended for four years, and so the details of my breakup fueled the flame of spirited teen gossip as graduation approached. Amid my hurt and humiliation, two special people, my science teacher and his wife, the school registrar, approached me one day and invited me aside to an out-of-the-way picnic table. There, away from inquisitive teenage eyes and ears, these two benevolent people let me talk while they listened.

To be sure, these teachers could have offered the expected simplistic platitudes about the immaturity of a high school romance and my brighter future after graduation, but they did not. They simply stayed close, expressing understanding without judgment. They didn't have to care, but they did, and I felt validated and worthwhile. Forever after, I considered them friends.

■ I moved the summer before my junior year of high school. I had a real hard time adjusting because I come from a dysfunctional family. Somehow Mr. G just knew. He figured out that I had an eating disorder and he took time out to talk with me and tell me he cared. He made me realize that my parents' problems were their own and that I needed to take care of myself. Overall, he befriended me at a time in my life when I felt like the world was against me—when I thought I was all alone. He showed me that teaching is an important profession and that teachers can have a tremendous impact on their students. (Bethany)

A number of years ago, one of my college students, Gwen, struggled with a problem that isolated and overwhelmed her. A normally vivacious young woman with sparkling eyes and charming smile, Gwen's depression took a toll, and she stopped coming to class. I became aware of the nature of Gwen's problem, and because we had a good relationship, I telephoned her and invited her off campus for lunch, not knowing what to expect but feeling committed to her. She agreed to go.

We met at a quiet, off-the-beaten-path café and chose a table outside, among flowering bougainvilleas that vined their way up a nearby brick wall. In this peaceful, rejuvenating setting, we discussed Gwen's own brick wall. I disclosed that I, too, had once faced a similar problem, and in the honest sharing, we effectively dismantled her isolation. Reflecting on the present with her, I explained that my problem had long ago faded to insignificance, like a blip on the radar screen of my life, and I expected the same for her.

Her charming smile slowly returned, and her downcast demeanor relaxed. We left the café, and in the course of time and renewal, Gwen's life rekindled with new meaning. Years later, her enormously successful teaching career overshadows what had previously threatened to choke her talents and potential. Our friendship continues still, the product of a journey often available to committed teacher and student travelers.

■ She had genuine concern for every student. During my sister's senior year, our father passed away, and Ms. B put together some inspirational poems for my sister when she graduated. That meant a lot more to her than all the gifts this teacher could have given her. I hope that when I become a teacher, I can have a relationship with my students like she did—as a teacher and a friend. (Jenna)

A MENTORING FRIEND

Students need to see teachers as growing people, teachers who are learning from their own mistakes and setbacks, honest in who they are, achieving new heights, and developing in character. Student learning, after all, is not isolated in a lesson objective. Students learn all the time from watching, listening, and experiencing life with a teacher-mentor who struggles and sets an example that students can consider and emulate as they tangle with their own setbacks on the road to mature adult life.

■ My band teacher had a disability, he lost a leg to cancer, but that didn't stop him. At the time I wore a back brace for scoliosis, so we instantly developed a bond and became friends. For some reason, the town opposed this new teacher and mounted a campaign against him. But one day he said, "I didn't let cancer get the best of me, and I'm not going to let this town get me down!" He won their support and has been the music teacher ever since. His influence skyrocketed me from last chair in my section to devoting my life to music education. (Christina)

The claim that teachers and students cannot be friends is premised on obvious ethical complexities and a misunderstanding of the nature of an appropriate teacher–student relationship (Klonoski 2003). True friendship between teachers and students takes time to develop and is based on goodness, honesty, and the best interest of students. A teacher friend lays the groundwork for trust as a student develops from a dependent to an independent learner and seeker of truth.

Such a friendship is not always warm and cuddly, but it is always authentic. To what, then, can one compare a teacher friend? A teacher friend is neither a peer nor a parent; instead, a real teacher friend is the best of both without being intrusive, inappropriate, or overbearing. A real teacher friend can relate to a student's journey having traveled the journey before, and with energy, forethought, and compassion, a real teacher friend guides the journey as a mentor with all the care and wisdom of one who has been there.

■ She wasn't one of these teachers who tried to impress students by being "cool" or "one of us." She was the same age as our moms, and the great thing about her was that she wasn't "a kid" and she wasn't a "mom" (a real drag in junior high!); she was the best of both. Junior high is a hard time for everyone—girls can be mean and hateful—boys can be thoughtless, and parents are starting to get on our nerves. Mrs. N was my confidante several times throughout junior high—she listened. Whether the problem was personal or scholastic, even after seventh grade, she was there. One always hears that you should talk to teachers when troubled—teachers are a guiding light, a source of information and assistance. She was this and more, a rare breed. The summer before my freshman year, she became ill. Anxious about a tough ninth-grade honors class, we were all counting on her to help us through like she saw us through her class, but she didn't make it back. She passed away before school started. It was the first time many of us had to deal with death, especially that of a close friend. There were about fifteen of us at her funeral. I made it through ninth grade, but I wished (and still do!) I had her there to see me through. (Danielle)

A teacher friend creates a climate in which all students can learn and grow as individuals. Simultaneously, a teacher friend enjoys students, valuing and listening to them. When students search for the right term with which to label this kind of teacher, the dictionary or thesaurus falls short of a unique and specific designation, and so students use the only word they can figure out, a word that comes closest to characterizing what they want to say about a valued teacher—and that word is *friend*.

In the sum of interactions, the big things a teacher does can make a big difference, and sometimes it's the accumulation of little things that pulse continuously with a clear message of friendship.

■ She sponsored our high school Quiz Bowl team. I remember one occasion when we were returning from a Quiz Bowl meet, and she had to step on the brakes suddenly. Her arm came over to make sure I didn't fly forward. I had my seat belt on, but she was just making sure I'd be alright. (Angela)

KEY IDEAS

✓ Understanding and adhering to appropriate boundaries builds friendly relationships with students that are based on trust.

✓ Valuing all students equally and referring to them by name convinces students that every class member is a teacher favorite.

✓ Shaping honest, appropriate mentoring relationships with students awak-
ens the kind of friendship that can last a lifetime.

II

BUILDING A LEARNING COMMUNITY

Imagine a scene of unleashed learning. Envision a classroom where students think and huddle to confer. Picture students engaged in tasks that intrigue the mind, using the best tools in mathematics, reading, science, physical education, English, technology, music, languages, art, or history to press toward individual and common goals. Imagine a network of students, linking their goals and outcomes together, feeding new understandings and larger purposes, amazing even the teacher—a partner in the classroom community.

Delivering instruction lockstep and scripted, with students in permanently tidy rows working in quiet solitary, may be easier to accomplish than the complicated, messier work of building a fluid community of learners ripe with variety and choice. Easier, yes, but certainly not as rewarding or fun.

Successful learning communities are not so different from successful societies. Both need community spirit, high expectations, and freedom to grow. Vibrant learning communities have an optimal chance to flourish in a climate that is safe, ordered, comfortable, and appealing—an environment where students and teachers trust one another enough to take academic risks. Building a learning community, like building a society, is not accomplished on the run or once and for all. It requires careful decisions, flexibility, commitment, and a lot of time. It is time well spent.

5

Classroom Ambience

■ Her classroom was the only classroom in the entire building to have curtains on all the windows! Usually windows in school have these plastic blinds, but she had taken the time to make red and white checked gingham curtains to hide these blinds. This gave the room a homey, comfortable look. (Lauren)

MY SPACE—WHOSE SPACE?

Building a learning community begins with a good look around school and classroom spaces to clarify who these spaces serve. I visited an award-winning middle school early one morning and wandered the halls shortly before classes began, stopping here and there to view glassed-in areas showcasing artifacts, projects, and photographs. The displays represented the lifeblood of this school—students, teachers, and activities—a diorama of smiling faces, athletic events, spirit days, and learning adventures—a welcoming, student-centered place.

Exploring further, the hallway ceiling unexpectedly caught my attention, where evenly spaced beams each listed the name of a state, its capital, the state flower, and the state bird. Turning right or left down another corridor, the beamed geography lesson continued with the names of world countries, their capitals, and dates of independence. Scanning the hallway beams, I acquired details about the world in just a few short minutes. Even this space, a commons intended for transport, invited students to learn.

The school had not yet sprung to life, yet classroom doors opened to my curious peek inside. What choices did the teachers and students make for their spaces? How did the spaces awaken interest and engagement? Many rooms displayed artistic student renderings—in spaces other than an art class. In others I saw large posters, clever quotations, listed procedures, artifact collections, and books—lots of them.

Some classrooms appeared organized as if the custodian had spent hours dusting and stacking. Other classrooms broadcasted intriguing disarray, as if students and teachers had unfinished work—don't touch—until the next day unfolds with new insights and progress. Walking the school halls early that morning offered a dynamic reminder that each classroom space in every school radiates a distinct personality, even in the absence of people.

■ After all of these years, I still vividly remember our classroom. As you entered our fourth-grade room, you instantly felt relaxed. Student writings and art projects decorated the walls and hung from the ceiling. We always had several live animals in our room (hamsters, guinea pigs, fish, and birds, all at one time!). I loved this because it gave us, as students, a sense of ownership. So often, as students, we assume that the classroom belongs to the teacher. By decorating in a comfortable manner that represents the students, this belief stops! (Jennifer)

A SENSE OF OWNERSHIP

Who owns the classroom? School districts? Teachers? Students? How is ownership rendered, and who holds the title? Who enjoys occupancy? In building an effective learning community, questions about classroom ownership are important to address at the outset.

Our eighteen-year-old Himalayan cat, Darby, thinks he owns our house. After all, he spends more time there than anyone else in our busy family, and he has selected several favorite spaces in which to curl up and nap for hours. His favorite spots include a dining room chair, the overstuffed family room couch, or the precise center spot atop the master room bed.

Because I dislike the remnants of his long white Himalayan hair, I bought Darby his own space at a pet store that specialized in feline comfort. I chose a small, round cat bed with curly lining akin to soft, freshly sheared sheep wool.

The cat bed, accurately sized for Darby's adult furry body and long fluffy tail, was perfect. I chose it, and I expected him to "own" it.

Arriving home, I removed the cat bed from its wrapper and placed it triumphantly in the corner of the family room near where Darby stood skittishly eyeing me and the new purchase. He hesitated, then sniffed the bed curiously but did not get in it. "Come on Darby, get in," I coaxed in my sweetest purring tone, "you will like it." He regarded me and yawned but didn't budge from his position.

Believing that I needed to introduce Darby more deliberately to his new space, I picked him up, put him in the cat bed, and then petted and held him there for a few seconds. His tense straining and meowing clearly signaled that he wanted out. I put him back in, and he got back out. I moved the cat bed to several of Darby's favorite areas of the house hoping to attract his interest, but day after day, Darby chose a spot to nap and shed, sometimes next to the cat bed but never in it.

Temporarily defeated, I hid the cat bed out of sight, hoping, at some later time, to reintroduce Darby to the bed more slowly. Several weeks later, I tried again. This time, I put the cat bed outside near Darby's favorite spot on the patio. I reasoned that, given the choice, Darby would select the soft, comfortable bed over the cold, hard concrete. No such luck. The bed remained outside for a week—unoccupied. After a last-ditch effort, I relegated the cat bed to storage to await the next garage sale. Darby simply did not feel any sense of ownership in this strange new space. I wonder if students feel the same when they enter a strange new classroom.

STRUCTURING SPACE

A sense of ownership cannot be forced on a student like a cat bed on an unwilling feline. How, then, can teachers go about the task of structuring a classroom space that welcomes students and invites them to a growing sense of ownership in all that transpires within? For schools and classrooms, the architectural elements—the walls, floors, and ceilings—are simply raw space, a shell (Ayers 2001). How does a teacher add life, dimension, and soul to four walls, a floor, and a ceiling to define the space with a unique and welcome personality that broadcasts that what happens here with students is important and valued? Without students who own the space, a classroom has a schedule but no soul. Filling classroom space in ways that honor students is no trivial task.

Veteran and new teachers alike approach a new school year by inspecting every nook of their empty classrooms and poking around each neglected storage area. It can be overwhelming. They think and plan, dream and design, and fill and toss. I recently received an e-mail from a former student just prior to his first year as a high school science teacher. With his permission, I share excerpts from his inaugural, reflective journey through his new classroom space.

■ I have spent the last nine days in my classroom getting acquainted with the ghosts of the past, adjusting my chair, and dreaming about the possibilities of the future. My classroom feels like a forgotten museum. There are many dead animals in jars (disgusting, they smell like death. I must get rid of them), machines and books that are at least forty years old, and filing cabinets filled with browning papers and copies of copies of copies that have been duplicated so many times they are starting to look fuzzy. There is a closet filled with some exciting, some exotic, and some very poisonous elements and compounds, a lab filled with science wares created before the invention of modern plastic. There are also many, many silent stories. I imagined what happened in this room and what it will be like when I leave it. I am coming in with hopes and dreams—the idealism of a new teacher. (Andy)

Discerning teachers envision a welcoming space, mining their own imagination and resources, and subsequently co-opting students to create the classroom personality. Like the television program *Extreme Makeover: Home Edition*, teacher and student "designers" can blueprint any classroom element—bulletin boards, walls, whiteboards, desks, and chairs—and enrich the classroom with captivating learning centers and displays, creating a space that students own now and still recall years later.

For students, classroom ownership is awakened in the heart and embraced like a gift to open and relish day after day. The appealing classroom fits comfortably, like a familiar favorite shoe, but it changes as well, offering surprises, like an unfolding kaleidoscope with its evolving visions and arrangements that appeal to the senses. No drab and lifeless place will suffice for a student-centered classroom. If students own their classroom, if they want to come and are reluctant to leave, they will assume growing responsibility for the activities that take place within.

BULLETIN BOARDS

■ My second-grade teacher had a bulletin board devoted to the month, and each person was responsible for two days. You could decorate your day any way you wanted! (Casey)

Drab cork-brown bulletin boards offer a convenient space to launch a co-operative design adventure and build classroom community. Rosenblum-Lowden (2000) suggests starting a school year with one bulletin board covered only in colored paper, left otherwise empty on the first day of school. The blank-slate bulletin board offers a useful opening canvas for any grade level—kindergarten through graduate school.

Teachers can foster an early sense of community among students with a get-acquainted or learning activity and display the result on the bulletin board. For example, elementary teachers might choose to capture students on camera the first day and engage them in preparing a bulletin board collage of pictures along with individual highlights of their favorite book, color, ice cream flavor, or holiday. Middle or high school students can design a mass crossword puzzle with personal clues for student detectives to unmask names and become acquainted.

■ My fifth-grade teacher inspired me the most. She made wonderful, informative bulletin boards for our classroom and various areas around the school. She let us help her with them. We all took great pride in our work. (Alyssa)

In my experience, elementary teachers, together with their students, tend to create beguiling and informative bulletin boards more often than do high school teachers. But bulletin boards are not just for children's delight. High school and college students have not outgrown the lure of eye-catching, attractive displays.

For example, in my graduate reading methods class, each of my students prepares a multicolored "found poetry" booklet linking inspiring phrases from favorite literary works and coupling them in poetic verse. Students illustrate the found poetry booklets with pictures and drawings. We share the results with each other and arrange the booklets in a bulletin board display. This not only introduces students to the content but also offers glimpses into the collective class personality for students in other classes to peruse.

WELCOME WALLS

■ He encouraged us to continue work on projects that we thoroughly enjoyed, sometimes for weeks afterward. In the event that a student had all of his or her work done, there were 500 task cards on the wall. Each card listed a small project to do, and these were recorded in a task card journal. If a student finished all 500, a rare feat, the student was given a special reward (like a free ice cream cone). (Nicholas)

Classroom wall space is another area to display student work, posters, and curriculum content, especially appealing when freshly posted and ever changing. On the other hand, without new student work and careful attention, wall displays dissolve into stale disregarded mainstays or tattered posters with long tears that hang loosely like lifeless marionette arms.

I recently noticed a first-grade classroom wall that depicted a large tree covered in bright red apples. While learning the long and short vowel sounds, each student prepared an apple for the short "a" sound and illustrated it with his or her name. The pint-sized students reached as high as they could to hang their apples on the huge tree. The title above the apple tree glowed with gold letters "You are the apple of my eye."

I visited a high school classroom and mingled with students to inquire about their projects displayed on every wall. One student described his fascinating word-study project. He had chosen a word from a list organized by his teacher. The list included words that evoked emotion, such as "love," "fear," "joy," and "freedom." His task involved using the chosen word as a cornerstone, selecting or drawing a picture to illustrate the word, locating a well-known literary passage that included the word, finding song lyrics that used the word, uncovering a famous quote that featured the word, and, finally, mounting his findings and analysis in a wall display.

After detailing his project in answer to my questions, he paused and sighed, "I never want to graduate—it is fun here—just look around." The classroom walls, filled with display boards, underscored and affirmed student thinking and creativity. The wall displays saturated the classroom and spilled out into the hallway, honoring student accomplishments in a way that other students, parents, and visitors could readily browse and appreciate.

Classroom walls can also be transformed into spaces that motivate a student who lacks interest in the course content. I know a biology teacher who enlisted an artistic student to paint a classroom wall mural of a whale against an ocean background in his classroom. Likewise, in a chemistry classroom, the teacher invited a student who did not particularly like chemistry but who loved art to paint a mural of the periodic table on the classroom wall.

With teacher encouragement, such students can learn content in ways that parallel their talent and interest profile. Teachers who engaged students in this way also had an agreement with the artisans that the wall could be repainted with new murals in succeeding years for an ever-changing learning canvas, liberating the classroom from depersonalized barren walls.

EYE-CATCHING WHITEBOARDS

■ One thing I loved about her classroom was the "quote for the day" on the board. Along with the quote was a word and definition. These little, yet significant, things made her classroom a very interesting environment. (Kelly)

At least one of any four classroom walls holds a blackboard or a whiteboard—generally the classroom focal point and conveyor of daily learning activities and assignments, a signal that important work is expected here. Typically, the whiteboard or blackboard is the first place that catches student attention because it is the one classroom area expected to change each day. Clever teachers make this area dazzle.

I regularly visited a Spanish classroom where the changing whiteboard portrayed an intriguing, hand-drawn caricature filling the middle of the board from top to bottom. The cartoon person engaged in an activity such as cooking, driving, or running. A large lettered sentence, written in Spanish, wrapped around the cartoon. Each time I visited the classroom, a new caricature on the board along with a new sentence piqued my interest.

Students congregated around the board before the opening bell rang, attempting to translate the Spanish sentence based on the drawing, an exercise that offered a natural segue into the day's lesson. The daily caricatures were easily traced from pictures projected on an overhead, confirming that even artistically challenged teachers can lure students and engage their minds with fascinating board art.

■ Every day when we came into class, there was a vocabulary word on the board. We all raced to look up the definition and copy it down because whoever did this first got a sticker. I got a lot of stickers! We had faith that if we got done with any activity early, she would have something else for us to do. Free time was a privilege and rarely granted. (Lauren)

A number of teachers signal that something important will happen in class by posting a daily agenda on the board. Students welcome this heads-up on what to expect. Agendas can be unrelentingly boring, with cursory lists of textbook pages to be covered and homework assignments to be completed along with due dates underlined in red. Although these lists are useful and necessary, agenda lists can also spark curiosity with creative labels.

After noting posted agendas during numerous K–12 classroom visits, I decided to try a regular posted agenda in my university classes. Even my serious doctoral students lightened up when listed agenda items included such headings as "think tank" to cue a class discussion or "campus hunt" to foreshadow an observation activity. In my experience, an ever-changing and creatively posted agenda encourages early attendance, arouses curiosity, and activates learning even before a bell signals the beginning of class.

MUSICAL CHAIRS—AND DESKS

■ The desks were never in the same place twice; we moved them according to the topics we discussed (sometimes in circles for unity or separate for diversity). At times we didn't use desks. This method produced confidence—every student was equal and important. (Erica)

Classroom ambience and an initial sense of student ownership begins with a student's table or desk. A few days before our granddaughter Casey started first grade, she and her parents visited the classroom. Casey's teacher had labeled each desk with a student's name. Tentatively exploring the room, Casey found her name and her space and recognized that she was welcome—she belonged here. This simple gesture planted the seeds of ownership for a hesitant first grader before school officially started.

In the larger picture, student desk arrangement indicates the nature of interaction expected among students and between the students and their teacher. Desk configurations answer the question, Does this teacher want to be in close proximity with students, welcoming dialogue and embracing connections as an eager collaborator in their learning? Or is business conducted in a more independent way that separates and divides teachers and learners? Indeed, classroom setup sends a clear, unspoken message to students and visitors.

Early in my teaching career, I substituted for the regular teacher in a third-grade classroom. Arriving early, I surveyed a most unusual and unwelcoming room arrangement. The teacher's desk occupied a place close to the front, hugging the whiteboard. The twenty-five student desks were stationed in constrained, straight rows at the back of the classroom, as close to the back wall as safely possible. A wide gulf divided the teacher's desk from the students' desks, like a vast waterless moat separating a king from the peasants. No equality here.

To me, the room arrangement sent a clear message—a visible space that separated teacher work from student needs. In effect, it said, "Don't bother me." Perhaps I misunderstood. Perhaps the teacher and students rendezvoused often within the moatlike space filling its vacuum with activities and camaraderie. I hoped so. Nevertheless, I clustered the student desks closer to mine for the time being. I reasoned that even a substitute teacher can configure temporary change.

There are many workable configurations for desks, tables, and chairs: learning pods with three or four students each, a center aisle with two sides facing the middle, U shape, V shape, squares, and circles. As long as students have an unobstructed view of the teacher, the board, and other learning areas, flexible seating arrangements that change from time to time offer a new beginning—at the start of a new semester, a new unit, or a new project.

When teachers change room arrangements occasionally, it injects an air of mystery and an element of surprise to an otherwise monotonous classroom. Students still like comfortable familiarity, so daily or weekly changes might be contrary to well-intentioned purposes. A teacher has to balance the dynamic environment, making it welcoming for all students. Over time, occasional change disengages classroom cliques and encourages students to widen their contacts and restore interaction with diverse groups.

■ The setting of the room was ever changing. The chairs were never where you expected them to be, and you were never expected to be in one chair. It was a student's dream: no seating chart, movement, always walking around the room, in and out of chairs, standing and sitting. Through all of this, order was maintained. By granting us freedom, we were given control over how the class was run. If we messed up, we lost our freedom. Why would we do that? (Sierra)

Recently, I learned a hard lesson—literally—about classroom chairs and movement about a classroom space. The incident occurred when I attended classes one day with a group of sixth graders, participating in their learning activities for the entire school day. The teachers and students expected and welcomed me into their cooperative groups. As an unofficial middle school student for a day, I sat in student chairs at student tables, read textbooks, joined student discussions, and moved from classroom to classroom, beginning the day with English.

Following a group of students inside for English class, the room lured me with painted warrior masks that circled the walls like extended valances with faces. The room arrangement featured eight round student tables, a variety of strategically located maps, a wide array of resource books, and a posted red, black, and green agenda that clarified our task for the day.

Joining my small group of sixth-grade classmates at a table near the back of the room, we commenced reading *The Adventures of Ulysses*. Sometime later, we traced Ulysses' journey on the nearby maps, discussed the background and meaning of such a lengthy journey, and drew a Viking ship. I learned new insights about Ulysses and his amazing adventure, but by the end of my full six-hour day as a middle school student, coursing through English, math, history, and science, I learned even more about student chairs.

Student chairs are not like teacher chairs. Student chairs are hard—very hard. No wonder middle school students are notoriously restless. Who can blame them? In fact, Knowles and Brown (2007) note the physical necessity for middle school students to move about a classroom, asserting that early adolescent tailbones are in the process of fusing, making it painful to sit for long periods of time in hard chairs. Likewise, consider the plight of younger children forced into chairs that leave their feet dangling a few inches from the floor. Imagine trying to balance your body all day long. Until schools can afford the luxury of plush, padded student chairs, in a variety of appropriate sizes, the opportunity to regularly stand and move about offers tailbone relief and a revived focus on learning.

■ We did not sit in our desk very much. We took our chairs and made circles or sat on the floor. She rewarded us by reading our favorite story, "Brer Rabbit," and she had a voice for each character. We really got involved with the story. She helped us make goals and check those goals. She had us write our goals for the month on slips of paper, then she kept them. We got them back a month later. This taught me a lot about working toward an outcome. She laughed with us, played games with us, and helped us reach goals. (Emily)

CLASSROOMS ALIVE

A teacher who attends to seating arrangements, walls, bulletin boards, and whiteboards before the school year begins outfits a classroom shell with the rudiments of personality. Taking the next step with thoughtfully designed learning and display areas breathes real life into a budding classroom personality.

I visited a fascinating elementary classroom where the teacher had constructed a two-story wooden learning area that students used for a reading loft. The loft included a lower level with puffy beanbag chairs, a cozy area rug, and reading lamps. To one side, a short ladder led to a railed loft that held cushions and pillows, scattered here and there, for cocooning with any of the books displayed on nearby shelves. The teacher rearranged the books regularly, like a merchandiser who encourages curiosity in overlooked literary finds. The well-worn, comfortable reading loft gave the children a unique way to practice literacy skills and a classroom home to enjoy.

A standout, dynamic classroom typically includes display areas for the hobbies and artifacts that both teachers and students prize. For young nature lovers, the opportunity to grow plants or flowers or to care for a classroom pet ensures memorable experiences. I've seen birds, snakes, guinea pigs, and mice. Students love them all. Recently, I visited a third-grade classroom where the student host welcomed me in and expectantly inquired if I wanted to see their recently hatched baby chickens, his eyes shining with owner's pride as he articulated the hatching process in detail.

Collective student and teacher relics from faraway travels and nearby exploration and objects that represent artistic, athletic, and musical talents or hobbies foster a growing sense of ownership and community. A couple of years ago, I visited a middle school mathematics classroom and noted a guitar leaning beside the teacher's desk—a prominent artifact that defined the personality of the teacher and this math class. The guitar awakened my imaginings of the teacher linking math concepts to lyrics and creating camaraderie among learners with algebra and geometry chants.

- The first thing that makes me laugh is that she was extremely musically gifted with an acoustic guitar. For holidays, she wrote songs that included everybody's name in the class in the song. The songs were funny and helped everybody feel a part of the class. (Nicolas)

A VISUAL FEAST

Like a person's home, the classroom is an expression of the interests, personality, and talents of the people within. With a little thought and collective imagination, students feel part of the class. Without a doubt, they feel ownership and pride in a classroom that features visual interest and highlights contributions from the students themselves. Something inside welcomes students, draws them into a learning community, and encourages their desire to stay.

Wong and Wong (1998) compare this kind of classroom to a favorite restaurant where the visual ambience suggests a fine dining experience. In such a restaurant, everything is ready, including the table, the music, the staff, and the food. Patrons want to return again and again. Similarly, for a classroom to feel comfortable and inviting, everything is ready: the seating, the walls, the board, the teacher, the learning areas, and the artifacts. A student can fill it, feel it, touch it, see it, experience it, and remember it.

KEY IDEAS

✓ Artfully highlighting classroom learning with picture displays, student projects, and artifact collections invites students in and convinces them to stay.

✓ Regularly changing displays and room arrangements, balancing the familiar with the novel, keeps a classroom fresh and inviting.

✓ Enlisting student creativity and input, as codesigners of the classroom space, enhances their sense of ownership.

Classroom Management

■ The year that I was in her class was her first year of teaching. She had to be scared out of her mind the first day of class in a new school, but you would never have known it to see her walk into the classroom on that day. She stood boldly in front of the class calling roll, and we all knew right away who was in charge. Nobody was going to get away with anything as long as she was around. Now that I think back on those days, I can see just how much we needed that kind of structure. (Sarah)

DREAMS AND REALITIES

Much has been written about classroom management. Perhaps this is because a well-managed classroom forms the framework of a safe learning community. Perhaps it is also because students who are preparing to teach (and some experienced teachers as well) report that classroom management is a pressing concern when they envision life as a teacher.

Quite simply, many new teachers are terrified of an inadequate ability to finesse an orderly learning environment. While students of teaching acquire instructional strategies in math, reading, and science, they crave the fortitude and confidence needed to inspire their students to respond with eagerness and engagement rather than indifference or disruption.

In truth, students of teaching have deep-down dreams—dreams that they will be ideal teachers with ideal classes. All teachers dream that their students will reflect none of the dysfunction from their families of origin but will meld into a new family of learners led by a capable teacher. These dreams can seem foolish in the harsh glare of classroom realities as teachers reconcile their dreams with a struggle to survive their early years in the classroom striving to organize rules, procedures, ambience, and lessons and still remain standing by 3:00 P.M. What we ask of teachers is no easy task.

Liston, Whitcomb, and Borko (2006) describe teaching as hard work, a daily grind to prepare stimulating lessons, diversify instruction, attend to bureaucratic accountability, accumulate resources, create an appealing environment, interact effectively with parents, ward off fatigue, and have some semblance of life beyond school.

Most experts suggest that grappling with these demands requires four or more years of experience to mark genuine progress in a new teacher's journey. Many new teachers have to muster all their energy reserves to overcome the fear—or the appearance of fear—when facing a classroom full of students on their own. Successful beginnings are neither easy nor happenstance.

STARTING WITH STRUCTURE

■ Her classroom management skills were impeccable. The first day of class, she laid out most of the rules. However, whenever assignments required special rules and procedures, she would explain them at the time they were needed (not beforehand). That way, we weren't bogged down with an excessive amount of rules to follow. (Sabrina)

For any teacher, new or experienced, the first few days of school are critical in establishing an orderly learning climate. Artfully engineering the numerous factors that converge on the first day of school makes all the difference between a successful beginning or the beginning of the end. A teacher's demeanor, organization, and preparation show—glaringly. A teacher's ability to establish a sense of leadership, coupled with caring interest, goes a long way toward setting the context for learning. There must be an understanding that every student is equally valued and that one person is responsible for orchestrating it all—the teacher. This is a monumental mission to be sure.

In describing order and structure, nature enthusiast Sam Campbell (1955) tells the story of Fiddlesticks and Freckles, twin fawns that Sam and his wife, Giny, raised after the mother doe, nicknamed Bobette, was blindsided late one night by a poacher with a bright light and a gun. Prior to her untimely death,

Bobette frolicked with her fawns, playing an animal form of hide-and-seek, providing hours of entertainment for Sam and Giny near their cabin in the Wisconsin woods.

Still, the stately doe understood the dangers lurking in the beautiful but threatening woods, and she taught Fiddlesticks and Freckles how to avoid threats from both animals and humans and prepare for their lives as maturing deer. Sam and Giny observed the daily lessons with fascination.

If the fawns got too close to humans, Bobette whistled and snorted repeatedly, sounding the familiar deer alarm. She proceeded to paw the earth with her feet and then trot to the woods and back again to face the pokey, curious fawns. The ritual between doe and fawns played out again and again each day—whistle and snort, paw the earth, stamp feet, trot to the woods, and return again to the fawns until the reluctant Fiddlesticks and Freckles regularly followed her cues.

Bobette consistently enforced her "deerly" crafted rules and procedures until the fawns complied habitually. Fiddlesticks, the one with long awkward legs, usually followed first with head erect, forward ears, and long bent legs strutting like a high-stepping drum major leading a parade. Freckles, the reticent spotted fawn, followed naively with innocent, big baby eyes that registered no fear.

Bobette loved the fawns without coddling them. She prepared them to cooperate with her and manage their own behavior in an unpredictable deer world. Following Bobette's untimely death (and the poacher's heavy fine), it took hours of patience and persistence for Sam and Giny to teach Fiddlesticks and Freckles a new procedure—how to drink milk from a bottle—to keep them from going hungry.

The deer family depicts a dual lesson applicable for successful classroom management and student self-management: *caring*, embodied in lighthearted playfulness, and *structured consistency*, necessary for introducing essential habits for smooth-flowing classroom life. The process of teaching and learning rules (the expected conduct to avoid disturbance or injury) and procedures (the accepted way to handle needs or tasks) is a necessary and not easily sidestepped rite of passage in any newly formed class.

Teachers may feel exasperated with the required time and consistent follow-through necessary, on a daily basis, to establish ordered routines in the early weeks of a school year. Some students will initially resist teachers' best intentions and efforts, testing their resolve. But steered with patience, kindness, and consistency, establishing fair rules and procedures eventually pays off in a functional, respectful classroom culture where students make good choices. This difficult jockeying for structure and routine cannot be ignored; it is a fact of classroom life, requiring vigilant attention.

DROPPING THE FACADE

■ He was an excellent high school teacher. It is difficult to explain why. I think it was because he cared so much for his students in a fatherly sort of way. He never had management problems for two reasons: (1) he was kind but firm, and (2) his class was very interesting. Even though he was firm, it was obvious he cared about us. He knew exactly when to be lenient and when not to be. I hope to find that balance and the ability to read students that he had. (Lily)

Some teachers fear that the challenging work of establishing classroom order requires a certain facade at first, like the worn-out, trite advice I learned thirty years ago: "Don't smile until Christmas"—a miserable way to spend the fall term for both teachers and students. Exploring classroom management beneath the facade, systematically rather than emotionally, uncovers more practical ways to simultaneously establish a well-managed classroom and be a warm, approachable teacher.

For example, effective teachers envision a classroom culture and set about to carefully plan and operationalize reasonable rules and procedures before the school year begins. When teachers interact genuinely with students and matter-of-factly describe effective classroom functioning on the first day, it signals a safe, stable haven.

Over time, if a teacher is consistent and fair in applying the rules and procedures, students come to understand the expectations in a particular classroom with a particular teacher (Stronge 2002; Wong and Wong 1998). In my visits to elementary, middle, and high school classrooms, I've observed that the same students behave differently in various classrooms, on the same day, depending on the particular teacher's expectations.

One telltale way to recognize a well-managed classroom is an organized list of a few (four or five) pertinent rules and procedures posted on the wall or clearly stated in a letter to parents or in a syllabus. Sometimes misbehavior occurs when students don't understand or remember exactly what they are supposed to be doing at any given time, and written expectations help alleviate misunderstandings.

Teachers who use positive language with written expectations set a better tone than those who use negative language. For example, stating a rule with positive language such as "Raise your hand to be recognized" rather than negative words such as "Don't talk without permission" reflects a tone of respect. Likewise, unfolding written and verbal procedures gradually over the first weeks of school affords students the time to practice and internalize them.

WITH-IT-NESS AND COMPOSURE

■ She always came to school looking like she should work in the finest law firm ever. She also had the composure of steel. In accounting, we always had the guys who sat in the back and talked about everything but accounting, and regardless of how many times she told them to be quiet, she never, ever raised her voice. She had a way of sort of smiling and saying, "That is enough." She kept their approval, and her class was in order. (Claire)

With-it-ness, an apt term coined by Kounin (1970), describes a teacher who is aware of the big picture in the classroom, including the "guys in the back of the room." This is a formidable task, characterized by many as akin to having eyes in the back of your head. With-it-ness is an essential teacher skill best developed through experience with a variety of students and situations.

Developing with-it-ness takes time, and often teachers must fall back and regroup, try something else, and recognize this skill as a work in progress. Teachers who develop with-it-ness progress from a narrow view of the classroom, as simply a context for delivering instruction, to a comprehensive view of everything that is happening in and around students, much like boring through a narrow tunnel to view the broader vista.

Some time ago, I observed a teacher circulating around his eighth-grade classroom to help students with their assigned task. A small group of students requested the teacher's assistance, so he crouched down beside the cluster of students, carefully attending to their questions. The teacher did a fine job of focusing narrowly on these students and meeting their needs. Meanwhile, the rest of the class slid off task and unraveled into chaos.

With-it-ness, for a teacher, means repeatedly scanning the classroom to the right and left and forward and backward, almost effortlessly, to cue all students that they are important and won't be ignored. A with-it teacher is fully aware of his surroundings, much like a juggler with flaming torches who carefully monitors each torch lest he lose track and get burned.

EMOTIONAL OBJECTIVITY

■ Talk about classroom management skills—Ms. S wrote the book, yet every child came back years later and thanked her. As for me, I was not her pet. In fact, I was a problem child at first. Sure, she quickly whipped me into shape, but I was not her favorite. She was the ultimate grade school teacher, the eye in the hurricane of elementary children. (Matthew)

Marzano (2003) suggests that with-it-ness be combined with an emotionally objective demeanor, like the calm eye of a hurricane. Emotional objectivity means that a teacher responds to student misbehavior in a straightforward manner without becoming upset or taking student misbehavior personally. Emotional objectivity does not require distance or detachment from students. It simply means carrying out classroom management tasks with composure and professionalism, like a teacher who has the "composure of steel" on the outside despite feelings on the inside.

Canter and Canter (2001) describe the process as "dropping down" emotionally. When teachers feel angry or frustrated, it is a big clue that something is about to compromise their role as classroom leaders. Teachers who quickly assess their feelings and consciously drop their emotional response to a lower key become decidedly calmer and better able to speak in measured ways. I've suggested that teachers view this process as a challenging game to play with their own emotions. A teacher friend disclosed that "there are certain kids who allow me to practice this game on a regular basis."

■ I don't really remember her ever getting angry, yelling, or punishing us. We all were well behaved because she kept our attention and interest and made learning fun. That's an important quality because it helped eliminate the need for discipline. No two days were ever the same. I probably learned more that year than any other year in elementary school. (Amanda)

Everyday, in busy classrooms, teachers are faced with potential inappropriate behavior requiring reflective judgment and, paradoxically, quick decisions about how to intervene. With-it-ness and insight, coupled with composure and professionalism, help teachers read students and situations, reframe a suspected problem, and balance the urge to react inappropriately with more healthy responses.

Not long ago, while presenting what I believed to be an important lecture, I noticed one of my students, Becky, take out a book—not the text readings for the day—and start leafing through the book as if intently searching for something. I had seen Becky reading the book before class, and I could only assume that she was bored with the lecture and had turned to something that interested her more at the moment.

In retrospect, it was a small distraction, but at the time it annoyed me as I floundered to keep my bearings in the lecture concepts. On and on Becky searched through the book and read, fixated and absorbed like Charlotte spinning a web. Miffed at her irksome behavior, I reflected on what I should do— say something, stop and wait, take the book, or ignore the irritation.

My presentation and my students' engagement seemed paramount to me at the time, gathering more importance as the minutes slipped by without Becky's attention. Although the class was relatively small, with students clustered closely at tables, the others scarcely gave Becky any notice at all. She was an above-average student, not particularly outstanding, but her work was consistent and acceptable. I decided to let the book incident pass without comment.

About ten minutes later, Becky raised one hand, smiling expectantly while holding her place in her book with the other hand. I recognized her, and she proceeded to share something she had remembered and found in her book that applied directly and insightfully to my presentation that day. Speechless, I felt foolish.

Notwithstanding my experience with Becky, a student's apparent off-task behavior can represent engagement with anything other than the lesson, and often a teacher just doesn't know. And so, in these situations, I ask myself two questions before responding to distractions. First, is the student distracting others and interfering with their learning? And, second, what is the student's typical class behavior? Is the seeming lack of engagement out of character or part of a pattern? In truth, teachers would give anything to read students accurately and consistently.

RECONCILING WITH STUDENTS

■ I entered high school a little bit afraid of the surroundings and the people. Mr. C put us all at ease from the start. He understood that we needed some intense structure in our lives. He made sure that we did our work. It was almost like you didn't want to disappoint him by not doing your homework. This is not to say that everyone in the class was a model student. There were those who tested him a few times. They would smart off to him or give him a bogus excuse for not having their homework. He had a way of turning the tables back on them without hurting them. (John)

Reconciling with misbehaving students avoids mutual embarrassment and maintains mutual respect. I learned that lesson early when my kindergarten teacher publicly embarrassed me. Enrolled in school scarcely two months, I was already in trouble. I probably deserved the consequence, although I don't recall the specific infraction, only the demeaning result.

It was October 31, Halloween, and the class party precipitated my misbehavior of some sort, likely stemming from childish silliness. Sometime during the day, the teacher wrote my name on the board in large block letters, as was her procedure with misbehaving students. My classmates stared at me for a time—some stifling giggles.

To compound my embarrassment, a school photographer took the official group picture of our class in full Halloween costume, positioning us in front of the blackboard with its decorative border and my name still prominently displayed. Ironically, I happened to wear a garish witch costume that Halloween. There I am in a tall, cone-shaped, wicked witch's hat standing in front of my naughty name. To this day, I have the pictorial evidence of my misbehavior—unforgiven and unresolved.

Years later, as a teacher, I faced one of my own misbehaving students, and I had a choice: expedite the consequence publicly or resolve it privately. The incident unfolded when I taught a high school culinary arts class for two weeks. The opportunity to teach this class allowed me to briefly abandon my university office and experience high school teaching again. The plan called for the regular teacher to be present in the classroom while I taught the class. Unexpectedly, however, the regular teacher was called out of town for two weeks, leaving me alone with sixteen students, a manageable group, even easy, or so I thought.

With Thanksgiving approaching and many varieties of juicy, crisp apples available, I decided to teach the students how to make apple pies. When I asked the students if they could name a variety of apple, the first responses were "red" and "green," so indeed, there was much to teach and learn. I began with eight varieties of apples, which the students tasted one by one. Next, they researched the Internet to explore which apple varieties bake well, and, finally, each student group developed a filling recipe based on personal taste and research.

Throughout the two weeks, I kept the student groups organized and busy, so classroom management was not an issue, with the exception of a boy I'll call "Dennis" because his mischievous antics and bids for attention reminded me of Dennis the Menace, the affable but aggravating cartoon character. To keep Dennis engaged in the content, I enlisted his help whenever feasible and assigned him a seat near the front of the classroom with an otherwise problem-free group.

I made an effort to get to know Dennis when we chatted before class (he always came early for food samples). During one of our conversations, Dennis described his after-school job at a popular deli sandwich shop. He explained, in no uncertain terms, how "the students from your university come in and eat sandwiches and take gobs of napkins and leave a mess all over the place." I expressed my understanding and sympathy. "They disrupt my work, and they are disrespectful," he added with finality.

A few days after my conversation with Dennis, the class groups made pie crusts to hold the apple filling they had prepared the previous day. Overseeing the students as they mixed and rolled pie dough required meticulous coordination on my part and more than the usual supervision. As class neared completion, I noticed that Dennis had formed a ball of pie dough that resembled a small baseball, and he quickly threw a curveball toward an unsuspecting student before I could intervene. Envisioning a free-for-all game of pie dough catch, I promptly collected every scrap of leftover dough from each group and quietly asked Dennis to sit down, separating him from the other students.

I completed the rounds of checking on groups, and soon the bell rang. Exiting the classroom, Dennis waved back at me with a mischievous smile, holding aloft another pie dough ball that he had somehow managed to confiscate and hide in his backpack. I stared after him in dumbfounded silence. I pictured Dennis retrieving the smuggled pie dough ball throughout the day to play contraband catch in other classes. What to do now?

The next day, the students were scheduled to eat their pies. Do I publicly ban Dennis from the much anticipated activity, sending him to the main office and detention? That would be the easy way out, of course, but what would he learn from the consequence? I pondered several scenarios. Ultimately, I took Dennis aside the next day prior to class.

Expecting the worst, he was taken aback when I smiled and asked him if he recalled our conversation when he described his job at the deli and how the university students made a mess, acted disrespectfully, and disrupted his work. We were silent for a few seconds—teacher and student reflecting. Finally, he broke the silence, "I think I know where this is going." I waited for the lesson to sink in. Presently, he looked up at me and said, "I didn't mean to disrupt the work of the class or to be disrespectful to you. I'm sorry. I won't do it again."

Dennis cooperated that day, eating his pie with enthusiasm and genial banter. A few weeks after I left the high school to return to my university classes, I received a thank-you card from the high school students complete with personal notes. Dennis thanked me too, adding a comment about baking the pies for his family's Thanksgiving dinner.

According to Henley (2006), discipline is less than ideal if it is merely a reaction to behavior problems. Understandably, a teacher's natural reaction may be to vent frustration, but that is never the most beneficial response to a misbehaving student. It precipitates escalating emotions rather than solving the problem. Instead, discipline must be proactive and educational. In this instance, letting Dennis recognize the parallel between his classroom behavior and his experience as a deli employee allowed him to reflect and visualize, resulting in a positive outcome for both of us.

A key factor in maintaining a well-ordered classroom is connecting with students in the way that Dennis and I connected during our private conversation about his behavior. Glasser (2000) suggests that problem behavior is exacerbated by poor connections with others: teachers, parents, or classmates. He recommends a reconciliation "connection room" instead of a punitive "detention room." In the connection room, students who disrupt teaching and learning can meet with an aide trained to offer opportunities for students to think or problem solve until the teacher can join the student. The objective is to eventually make a positive and lasting connection with the student.

In retrospect, prevention is another key factor in maintaining a well-ordered classroom that is efficient and organized with little time left for misbehavior. For example, the transitions from one classroom activity to another, like transitioning from rolling pie dough to adding filling to baking, are times when students are especially prone to misbehavior. Vulnerable transitions also occur when students are asked to move about the classroom from one setting to another.

Students in close proximity without a specific task or set routine for changes are tempted to interact in ways that are inconsistent with classroom expectations. Teachers who pay close attention to transitions, ensuring that they are smooth and efficient, prevent potential classroom difficulties. For me, a more organized set of transition steps and signals in the pie-making lesson might have prevented the pie dough catch fiasco. Experience is a good teacher of teachers.

JUSTICE AND MERCY

■ My fifth-grade teacher was extremely personable and friendly and at the same time earned the respect of his students. He gained respect in subtle ways by presenting clear objectives and following through on consequences and reinforcements. The students realized that he meant what he said, and we were always aware of the consequences of our actions. (Stephanie)

Teachers know that rules and procedures are essential to efficient classroom functioning. Consistent follow-through with consequences for misbehavior establishes habits that govern class structure and student security. Regardless, adhering to rules and procedures and meting out consequences are not always clear-cut and simple. There are times when even well-intentioned procedures miscarry in heartrending ways.

The occasional disconnect between rules and consequences hit home when our son, Kevin, was in third grade with a teacher noted for detachment rather than warmth or compassion (the same teacher for whom I substituted with the waterless moat in her classroom). One of her rules, well known and regularly enforced, dictated that if she left the classroom for a minute or two, students were to remain in their seats, under the direction of a room monitor. If any student was caught out of his seat, he had to lay his head on his desk with eyes hidden.

One day, when his teacher stepped out of the classroom, Kevin slipped out of his seat. He didn't intend to misbehave in the spirit of the rule; nevertheless, he clearly misbehaved in the letter of the rule. It was February 14, Valentine's Day, and Kevin had decided to give his teacher a valentine, leaving his seat to place the card on her desk—the only time when he could do so anonymously. This teacher, who was not his favorite, would likely receive few, if any, valentines, so the small valentine, created by a child, was a thoughtful gesture.

When the teacher returned to the classroom, she caught Kevin sneaking back into his seat. She commanded Kevin to bury his head on his desk. Within the next few minutes, of course, the teacher noticed her only valentine placed carefully atop other papers on her desk and asked, "Who gave me this valentine?" With head still buried on his desk, Kevin raised his hand and quietly answered, "I did."

As expected, the consequence remained in place, consistently administered. But this story illustrates that often there are shades of gray in a student's behavior—things we don't fully know and backgrounds and attitudes we don't fully understand. All teachers, even those who are warm and caring, make these mistakes.

Feelings of sorrow and guilt when enforcing rules and consequences are part of a teacher's sojourn, even when the consequences seem justified. Did I do the right thing? is a question ever close to a teacher's heart. It helps to remember that respect, metered judgment, and mercy are useful teacher tools and dispositions. It helps to remember, too, that teachers can apologize. Students are remarkably resilient when regarded and respected in this way.

DAILY MOOD

We would do well to remember that a teacher is one of the most important adults in a student's life. When implementing rules, procedures, and consequences, all essential to a well-organized learning community, psychologist and teacher Haim Ginott (1972) reminds us to carefully consider and model the behavior we would like to see in our students:

> I am the decisive element in the classroom. It's my personal approach that creates the climate. It's my daily mood that makes the weather. As a teacher, I possess a tremendous power to make a child's life miserable or joyous. I can be a tool of torture or an instrument of inspiration. I can humiliate or humor, hurt or heal. In all situations it is my response that decides whether a crisis will be escalated and a child humanized or de-humanized. (13)

KEY IDEAS

✓ Careful thought to a few basic rules and procedures, developed before the school year begins and clearly stated on day one, establishes harmony and a positive vision for classroom life.

✓ Students respond well to consistency from day one; consistent follow-through fosters appropriate habits of functioning and cultivates a secure learning community.

✓ Justice mingled with grace and private reconciliation preserves student dignity and fosters mutual respect.

✓ Classroom management takes years to master, and even then, a challenging new group will require renewed, vigilant efforts.

7

Learning Activities

■ To this day all I can draw are stick people, but for the three years she was my art teacher, she had me making masterpieces. I never heard a negative comment or remark from her. She deeply believed in developing the talents each child had. (Alexis)

GETTING ACTIVE

From art masterpieces to historical plays to science explorations, the myriad things that students do in classrooms are tagged learning activities. Linger, if you will, on the term *activities* and its root word *active;* imagine what an active classroom looks like and feels like. Contrast that image with my invented word, *passivities,* to describe more tedious classroom pursuits. The word *passivities,* with its unappealing root, *passive,* sounds absurd, evoking images of students glued in a quagmire of contrived, sedentary tasks. With each new task, once luminous eyes dim rapidly like burned out lightbulbs.

While it is true that students benefit from both active and passive learning, most classroom schedules devote an inordinate amount of time to teachers actively instructing and students passively receiving or passively sitting to complete mundane tasks. Teachers who regularly shake things up and engage students in actively considering big ideas and persisting through projects discover the ennobling power of active learning as a novel and intensely satisfying complement to more passive classroom pursuits.

■ Before this teacher I had no interest in social studies. This changed dramatically after I took his American government class. We did a lot of cooperative work, including discussion and role playing. We used the newspaper and analyzed editorials. We conducted mock trials with everyone held responsible for an assigned part. We partnered in a videotaping project of a decade that included news events. He taught in such a way that all students participated, not just the "smart" ones! He kept us actively interested in topics that had the potential to be very dry. (Ariana)

I fully embraced the concept *active* when I pet-sat for our daughter's dog, Maya. Part of my caretaking responsibility included taking Maya, a gray Lhasa Apso, on her daily walk. As a lifelong cat owner, I had never walked a dog or any pet for that matter. So, with cautious optimism, I clumsily clipped on Maya's leash and ventured out to her favorite destination, a nearby dog park where dogs are welcome and free to explore and romp with other dogs in a large fenced area.

Arriving near the street crossing that accessed the park, Maya suddenly lurched, taking off in a run with me dragging along behind. Once inside the fence, Maya strained to be unleashed, and, once free, she raced off to meet a white poodle. Maya proceeded to chase the sophisticated poodle, then spin around and run, glancing back at the poodle in pursuit.

Back and forth this ritual continued as each dog investigated every inch of the park. Before long, Maya stuck her nose through the chain-link fence to greet a German shepherd approaching with its owner. Maya's unleashed enthusiasm galvanized her diverse peers to become discovery explorers. As with all dogs, Maya has basic activity needs, the freedom to move about, explore, and interact with other dogs. Passive, isolated strolls tethered to a master's leash do not suffice.

Students who languish in a boring classroom are not too far removed from a leashed dog. They simply want to break away from monotony and do something active. Reflecting on this notion, a teacher friend disclosed her eighth grader's comment during a long, hot summer school class period. With puppy dog eyes, the boy pleaded, "I just can't do it. I just can't sit still. It hurts to sit here." Students have a valid point about long, dragging class periods choked with remedial, passive seat work. In such classes, students become like coiled springs waiting for the signal to bolt.

Ask most any child about a favored school activity, and the answer is likely to be recess. No wonder. Activity dominates the terrain of the playground. A discerning teacher who designs ways to harness student passion for activity and connect it in meaningful ways to the curriculum can transform a learning community and powerfully impact student potential.

■ She took the time to help us to understand how each subject held importance in our lives. For example, we took nature walks along a creek that ran next to the school. We looked for fossils in the creek bed or for a variety of plant species and talked about photosynthesis. We took a snack break or had a picnic lunch. Afterward, we broke up into teams of two or three and looked for specimens on our own. We had so much fun that we often didn't realize how much we were learning. (Jasmine)

In a similar outdoor learning example, a colleague recounted his experience teaching the solar system to his fourth-grade students. They depicted the school as the sun. Next, they placed the planets at appropriate distances with Mercury almost touching the school. By the time they had paced off Venus, Earth, and started on Mars, they had ventured a great distance from the school, and the students concluded that they could spend all day walking before arriving at Neptune. These students learned science while actively absorbing the vast splendor of nature, where nature really happens, outdoors.

When teachers get active with the curriculum, the dynamics of learning fundamentally change. In wearisome, exclusively sedentary classrooms, there comes a point when students stagnate like mental hourglasses measuring time incrementally, class after class, like sifting sand, waiting to be upended only to start over. Rather, active learning, if taken seriously in classrooms, encircles students in a community characterized by exploring, questioning, walking, researching, discussing, acting, inventing, choosing, presenting, creating, assembling, and illustrating.

■ I remember learning a great deal from my seventh-grade creative writing teacher. Instead of just having us write stories and turn them in, she had us make our stories into plays. We invited other creative writing classes to come and watch, and then we would go and watch their plays. This way we learned many different writing styles without having to read a lot of boring textbooks. We worked hard to make our stories creative so that ours would be picked to become a play. This inspired us to keep writing. (Madeline)

BENEFITS OF ACTIVE LEARNING

Active learning has a remarkable impact on thinking and remembering. John Dewey (1916), an early proponent of active learning concepts, found that students cannot be tangibly active without actively thinking. Over time, the process of doing and thinking floods an activity with meaning and significance in the mind. The thinking process, fueled through meaningful activity, transforms and strengthens networks in the brain, enabling students to construct new understandings. Subsequently, strong neural networks recharge and organize memory storage and retrieval.

To illustrate the range of contexts related to learning and memory, Dale (1969) developed the Cone of Experience, familiar, but worth careful reflection. Dale asserted that two weeks following exposure to new information, we remember a percentage of what we encounter, depending on the mode of our experience (see table 7.1).

A student can see or hear information without being actively engaged in thinking about it or using it in some meaningful way. Like our students, we have each experienced a wandering mind or absentminded thinking when listening passively to others present information. On the other hand, students who assume speaking, doing, and interactive teaching roles find that the ambitious undertaking requires not only active involvement but also active thinking. There is no compelling reason for teachers to do all the teaching.

Table 7.1. Cone of Experience

Information	Percentage Recall after Two Weeks
What we read	10
What we hear	20
What we see	30
What we see and hear	50
What we say	70
What we do and say	90

Source: Dale (1969).

Classroom learning activities, taken literally as active experiences, result in adventures like acting out a concept in a dramatic presentation, exploring an idea through simulation, designing a project, or teaching a concept to someone else. The concept is more likely remembered based on deeper levels of processing. Active involvement is even more meaningful when students sense a connection between what they do in school and their lives outside of school. In other words, learning is best conducted when it is integrated and not isolated from real life.

REAL-LIFE LEARNING

■ My sixth-grade art teacher stands out in my mind. He actually taught us real things about art, not just Christmas projects and St. Patrick's Day clovers. I remember him being extremely happy and energetic. He encouraged us, no matter what, and we moved at a fast pace. He gave me my first glimpse of art as a serious real-life subject. (Olivia)

I better understood the fundamental difference between ordinary learning and real-life learning when I taught high school home economics early in my career. My foods and nutrition class generally misunderstood my expectations of this as a serious subject, and often my goals and my students' goals seemed at odds. On the one hand, I wanted my students to embrace the significance of food preparation for its nutrition, color, texture, variety, and presentation. However, my students' prime interest in the class consisted of inviting friends to join them in devouring their culinary experiments. To them, the class resembled a series of grand parties.

Partway into the school year, our class priorities changed when a tragedy stunned our school family. A local college student and brother to three of our high school students died in a car accident. Deeply saddened, students clustered in protective flanks around each other and the three remaining brothers. Many students had not dealt with death at such a young age, and for a time, they could not focus on schoolwork.

At this juncture, I decided to engage my students in a gesture of kindness to help us all cope with this crisis. I proposed that our class prepare a full meal for the grieving family. After all, I reasoned that relatives would soon arrive in town and that, as a practical matter, they would need food. My students' enthusiasm to serve the family refocused their sorrow in a positive way.

As menu plans and food preparation commenced, my students' demeanor and attitude changed dramatically. Food preparation elements such as color, nutrition, balance, and presentation became as important to them as did taste. Everything they had learned converged in this real-life opportunity to provide for the needs of others. The family's grateful appreciation for this simple act of service helped my students heal and internalize a sense of civic responsibility. I recognized that service cannot be taught in the abstract—it can only be experienced.

School is not an isolated place, shut off from the real world. Good teachers penetrate beyond school borders to encompass the community and the broader world. Travel and community involvement noticeably inform any teacher's repertoire of experience, and, if carried into the classroom, these experiences inspire students with a broader vision of life, the world, and fascinating people and cultures.

■ The thing I remember was the time we cooked an authentic Guatemalan dinner. She had lived in Guatemala for ten years, and she tied this into our course work, culminating in the dinner. This sticks out in my mind because she gave us an appreciation of another culture, and she did this because it was intuitively right, not because the administration said our classroom needed to be multicultural. This made her a great teacher. She did what was right for the students. (Austin)

BASIC SKILLS AND CREATIVITY

Some might argue that active, real-life learning experiences divert time and attention away from essential basic skills instruction like grammar, phonics, and computation. Indeed, Microsoft mogul Bill Gates, who, along with his wife, established the Bill and Melinda Gates Foundation to fund education projects, suggested in a *Parade* magazine article in 2007, "If you don't know how to read, it doesn't matter how creative you are." He makes an important point: students must have basic skills as a solid foundation for additional study.

Of course, state mandates, curriculum guides, and standardized tests all demand basic skill instruction. In the face of this challenge, effective teachers discover creative ways to balance the delicate seesaw between basic skill instruction and project-based activities. Such teachers expend enormous effort connecting with student interest without sacrificing foundational learning.

Instead of limiting the curriculum, memorable teachers somehow magically maneuver the phonics drills, grammar exercises, and practice sets, integrating these basic skills with larger purposes, broader content, and real life.

■ We learned basic material about writing and literature, but he mixed it with stories about his involvement with the theater. He incorporated many different learning methods—reading, writing, acting, discussing, predicting. He allowed for our own artistic interpretations of works. Furthermore, he offered his interpretations and shared his own writing, which showed us that "ordinary" people can be creative and publish. He never condemned work as long as it was sincere, genuine, and backed with effort and reasons for its validity. (Melissa)

PRIMARY RESOURCES

Real-world active study necessitates real-world primary resources. Although textbooks are neat and tidy summaries for student consumption, they can be patently dull with narrow and synthesized viewpoints. Textbooks, useful as they are, are secondary resources created by someone else. Primary resources are firsthand learning materials that can be examined and applied to extend the basic skill concepts gleaned and synthesized from textbooks.

Examples of primary resources to integrate with a variety of subject areas include architectural blueprints, photographs, fine art, tombstones, real people, nature, letters, statues, bridges, music, maps, advertisements, cookbooks, machines, documents, field trips, animals, athletic event documentaries, apprenticing, gardens, supermarkets, and newspapers. This short list barely scratches the surface of primary resources. The key is to touch and experience life as applied to textbook concepts but decidedly carry student learning beyond a textbook.

■ In his social problems class, he handed out a textbook the first day, a textbook that was never opened by his students. He said, "It's merely procedure; this book was written by stiffs. If we're going to learn, we're going to learn about cool stuff." And believe me, we did. He had unlimited resources, files upon files of magazine articles, newspaper cutouts, video recordings, and gobs of books. He was a fiend for this

type of information. We spent every week on a different subject (topics like child abuse, serial killers, rape, white-collar crime, police
abuse, and many other topics). Going to his class was fun, a nice
break from trigonometry and all that other crap. (James)

With my newer conception of primary resources and how such resources
can transform a classroom, I might have included history as one of my teaching areas if I had a second opportunity to choose. In recent years, I have
relished a slew of historical biographies, extensive travel at home and abroad,
absorbing cultural artifact collections, and my great grandmother's insightful
diary from 1886.

Back in my school days, however, my natural inclination for history deteri-
orated with a steady diet of dry textbooks, displaced renderings of the real
world, and grim lists of dead people accompanied by names and dates to
memorize. Like many students before and since, I don't recall delving deeper
into history beyond the textbook. I often wondered about the real people and
backstories behind those glossy pages and pictures but was offered little else
for studying the fascinating course of world events.

MULTIPLE CAPACITIES FOR LEARNING

■ He liked to do nontraditional things, like taking us on a nature walk
to show the biological diversity in our own territory. He also related
basic geometric principles to everyday life. He brought in building
blocks and had students build a playhouse using simple geometric
equations. For geography, he had students put their finger on the
globe and spin it, and wherever it stopped, that place would be the
basis for the lesson. He started by asking the class what they knew
about the place and went from there. (Stephanie)

Students who explore topics in nontraditional ways and incorporate activities such as designing, building, investigating, observing, acting, and singing
often amaze teachers—and themselves—with the extent of their capacity to
learn in novel ways. Neuropsychologist and educator Howard Gardner (1983)
transformed our understanding of how diverse students learn with his comprehensive framework for human intelligence. Historically, educators viewed

Table 7.2. Multiple Intelligences in the Classroom

Intellectual Capacity	Pathway to Learning	Active Learning Example
Verbal linguistic	Words	Write stories and debate ideas
Logical mathematical	Numbers and reasoning	Analyze numbers and concepts
Visual spatial	Pictures and graphs	Draw concept illustrations
Bodily kinesthetic	Movement	Create plays to act concepts
Musical	Music and recordings	Create concept songs
Interpersonal	Social interaction	Group projects and discussions
Intrapersonal	Self-reflection	Journal responses and ideas
Naturalist	Natural world	Collect data from nature

Source: Armstrong (2000).

school intelligence as one dimensional, adhering to a narrow conception of the most capable students as verbally and mathematically more gifted than other students. Over time, these intellectual capacities became the most touted and valued capacities in school, and thus students were pressed to conform.

Gardner's theory of multiple intelligences took issue with a narrow view of intelligence and advanced a spectrum of seven distinct intellectual capacities. The seven intelligences, initially posited in the theory, were later expanded to eight, and Gardner has hinted at a ninth intelligence. Numerous books and online sources have extensively explored the theory and its practical classroom application for teachers and students. Table 7.2 enumerates Gardner's eight identified intelligences along with their learning pathways and a corresponding classroom activity example.

Collectively, students respond to this liberated conception of intelligence because multiple methods for learning open multiple ways to remember the distinguishing characteristics of content under study. In addition, the methods correlate with a wider range of student interests, allowing more students to shine in an otherwise dull classroom.

■ He taught psychology by using visual and auditory learning strategies to tap the many different styles of each child. He tapped into the visual side by bringing his one-year-old daughter into the class to show us different types of motor skills for a child at this age. He tapped into our auditory side by bringing in music, making us listen to the words, and asking us to recognize certain psychological terms in the music. (Angel)

How can a teacher figure out a particular student's preferred pathway to learning? One way is to keep a notebook with a page for each student that includes brief observations noted here and there about particular students' responses to different learning activities. It is well worth integrating a variety of learning pathways to observe how students variously respond, often in ways similar to how they learn something new outside the classroom. Teachers might also simply ask students to write a list of what they like to do after school—other than homework (e.g., drawing, dancing, building, collecting, talking, writing, acting, and computer activities).

To recognize the full power of multiple intelligences, one need only step back and observe how young children learn—how they effervesce with curiosity, rapid-fire questions, a myriad of guess-what tales, an assortment of crayon renderings, and a heap of clever theories about life. In any sizable group of young carefree children, all eight multiple intelligences bubble like a fountain, and children, like gigantic sponges, absorb everything they can possibly learn, and they do so in multiple ways.

For example, when our granddaughter Casey completed kindergarten, her teacher held a graduation ceremony. The young graduates, dressed in white caps and gowns, marched down the auditorium aisle and assembled on the platform in a large semicircle. The ceremony opened with a class video projected on two large screens, accompanied by spirited music.

Most of Casey's classmates watched the video, listening quietly on this formal occasion. Meanwhile, Casey tapped her feet, clapped her hands, and mouthed the lyrics, syncing the music and the video with her subtle but animated gestures. Casey continued, absorbed in rhythm throughout the fifteen-minute video.

Observing her in this context, I considered the possibility that Casey might enjoy learning kinesthetically—that is, by moving. To be sure, she learns in other ways as well; indeed, all students learn by combining their intellectual capacities, as needed, for the task at hand. Still, Casey revealed her interest in learning through movement when she started first grade and lamented "another six hours of sitting." She is no different from other students who like to learn in novel ways.

■ I found it interesting when our teacher used an audiotape of Beethoven's Fifth Symphony along with several overhead presentations to get the class interested in Euclid's *Fifth Book of Elements*. It helped me learn. (David)

Not long ago, I observed a teacher engage his diverse seventh graders with a marvelous repertoire of multiple intelligence strategies. Arriving at his classroom, I noticed a large colored chalk drawing of a human heart on the sidewalk, just outside the door. The accurate and detailed rendering included the aorta, ventricles, atriums, valves, arteries, and veins.

Following a brief introduction, the seventh graders lined up outside, and each meandered through the heart like so many blood cells pumping rhythmically through its chambers—learning science, nontraditionally, through movement. Afterward, student triad groups examined halved red peppers that represented the human heart, and they labeled the chambers using paper pennants and toothpicks. The teacher finished the lesson with a primary resource, a pig heart prominently displayed and prompting a buzz of interest among the student biologists as they examined the formaldehyde pig heart. Students engaged in several multiple intelligence strategies in order to learn; kinesthetic, visual, spatial, and interpersonal. Impressive.

LEARNING COOPERATIVELY

■ We completed many projects with two or three other students (we had the same cooperative groups at least a semester—sometimes a year). For example, our group read and critiqued each other's writing. We studied vocabulary words and took tests in groups, and we later wrote stories that incorporated at least twenty-five words. (Jacqueline)

The interpersonal component of multiple intelligences is commonly called cooperative learning—a well-recognized and socially dynamic way to study that accentuates cooperative synergy rather than competitive divisions. Numerous educators, including Johnson, Johnson, and Holubec (2007), offer guidelines for organizing cooperative learning step-by-step, including assigning group roles, structuring group interdependence toward a common goal, requiring individual accountability, teaching cooperative behaviors, and processing how well groups achieve their goals. Vigilant adherence to these elements, along with classroom practice, creates a climate for seamless group functioning and successful learning outcomes.

Notions about working cooperatively in groups have changed dramatically since I attended elementary and high school in the 1950s and 1960s. In those days, students worked independently, sitting dormantly and silently at desks to complete tasks—alone. Working with other students raised suspicions of cheating, so working alone trumped cooperative work in any classroom.

I do recall a "one-time-only" cooperative project that allowed me to work with a classmate. Mr. Adams, my sixth-grade teacher, assigned pairs to develop reports on South American countries. I worked feverishly with my partner on our poster of Uruguay, labeling the important cities and resources, gathering relevant artifacts, and carefully coordinating it all for class display. I've long forgotten other class assignments but still remember the interaction with Barbara, my cooperative learning partner, and our sense of accomplishment. Real life necessitates interaction with other people—at work, in a marriage, and in a neighborhood. Wise teachers use cooperative learning strategies to prepare students along the way.

■ She had us work together often, which I think is important. We worked on a lot of school plays in cooperative groups. All the parents came and friends. We learned how to work with each other. It allowed us to socialize and build friendships easier than in other classes. It also gave us a sense of accomplishment and self-esteem (plays were hard work). We did do academic work, but it was the other stuff that made her special. (Michael)

Michael suggested that his class did "academic work," but the "other stuff" they did made his teacher special to him. Paradoxically, when students enjoy active learning, they may not recognize that it is, indeed, academic work just structured differently and more actively than other, more passive learning tasks.

INTERDISCIPLINARY INSTRUCTION

■ Two of my high school teachers stand out head and shoulders above the rest. These two taught a two-hour block class combining American history, literature, and composition. They divided the course material into thematic units, and we explored the history, literature, art, and music of the period. I remember enjoying how we learned the material in context, like how the history impacted the popular music of the time. (Lindsey)

Cooperative learning reaches new levels when several teachers, along with their students, cooperate in an interdisciplinary activity that blurs the artificial boundaries between their subject areas. I encountered an exemplary interdisciplinary, cooperative activity several years ago during a cold Minnesota winter.

Two middle school teachers, representing science and English, harnessed the state's long cold winters to engage their students in a cooperative interdisciplinary experience with the theme "Survival" to contextualize students' thinking. The science teacher hosted her students on a field trip to the snow-covered Minnesota wilderness so students could study survival skills firsthand rather than rely solely on the textbook for information. Student groups built an igloo, stayed overnight in their Eskimo-style home, and tested their coordination after dipping their arms in vats of ice water.

Back in class, the science student groups researched the necessities for survival kits, testing several brands of candles to determine which brand would burn the longest. Students brainstormed a list of items most useful for survival kits, and each student prepared a personal kit including, among other items, coins, candy, water, batteries, tape, and a flashlight.

Meanwhile, in English class, the same student groups read *Julie of the Wolves* (George 1972), which unfurls the adventure of an Eskimo girl lost in the Alaskan tundra without food or a compass. Julie struggles to survive and ultimately saves her life by communicating with a pack of arctic wolves. Reading, reflective journaling, and cooperative group discussions prompted research questions about wildlife among the wolves and an exploratory field trip to a nature center.

All told, these two teachers were so jazzed that they prepared a video of their students' learning experiences to share with other teachers at their school, and their students made me a practical survival kit to keep in my car. This active interdisciplinary learning experience offered students explicit connections between otherwise discrete subject areas.

CHOICES AND CONTROL

■ He allowed students to express themselves in a very creative manner. For example, I remember doing a section on poetry, and he allowed us to act out the poem in any way we wanted, using any props we wanted. This activity made what is usually a boring subject very fun, and I remember learning so much poetry from watching the other students. He did activities like this all the time. (Gabrielle)

Teachers who discover their students' ideas and interests experience a particular joy and satisfaction understood only by educators. Pursuing student interests requires time and effort because interests among a typical student group are substantially varied and infinite. Allowing students to have choices in their curriculum and activities is a good way to uncover hidden interests and build a passionate and productive learning community. Choices encourage students with a sense of responsibility for their own learning, a desire to accomplish something worthwhile, and a feeling of control over their products and outcomes.

Having been an advocate of student choice and autonomy as a motivating force in the classroom (Ryan and Deci 2006), I decided to take a risk with one of my teacher education courses by encouraging my students to choose their own major project. I couldn't predict the outcome. Nevertheless, I wanted to try an edgy, autonomous approach with my teaching methods students who represented a variety of content areas including science, mathematics, physical education, history, and English.

On the first day of class, I reminded students that they were experts in their respective subject areas but suggested that there might be something within their subject area that they still wanted to learn. If they pursued that knowledge gap, it might prop up their teaching confidence. They readily agreed.

I structured a required number of study hours, asked for a study plan and weekly e-mail updates, but allowed them complete autonomy in choosing what they wanted to learn about their subject area and how they wanted to learn it. The students amazed me with their passion and energy, verbalizing this as their most useful higher-education learning opportunity.

I recall one project in particular, that of an English major who admitted that although he had majored in English, he had somehow progressed to graduate school without having read any of Shakespeare's works. For his study project, he chose to read three complete works of Shakespeare and prepare student activities to accompany each work that he could later use when he taught these works to high school students. He, along with other students, welcomed this opportunity to grow professionally through autonomy and control of their own learning.

■ She was simply incredible. She taught above and beyond the great literary works, grammar points, and how to write. She taught us about creativity, organization, and life. We did a huge "research" paper where we did the research and wrote on whatever topics we chose (example: How can I help save the earth?). The best part was the freedom allowed in writing the piece—mine ended up being a science fiction story about how the world had changed due to environmental problems. These papers were a part of my life—not just an assignment. Besides that, our journalism class put out a literary magazine, put on an entire recorded production that played on a local telethon, printed a biweekly newspaper, and produced the yearbook with less than twenty students. (Jacqueline)

WHAT STUDENTS KNOW

Students know something about the rhythm of a robust classroom: a transformative classroom that radiates student ideas, interests, and talents. They offer a clear appeal to teachers—let us do something: something active, something real life, something that showcases our unique capacities. Engage us as we are now and help us grow into all that we can be. The benefits are unlimited, surprising, and deeply fulfilling. I find that I am most alert and alive when a class period exceeds my expectations, when students spin a broad range of ideas and originate a startling array of culminating products. Without a doubt, engaged students ignite sparks that warm and satisfy a teacher's soul and their own as well.

■ She varied her teaching methods so we didn't get bored. There was a lot of student involvement. We acted out plays, we did group projects, and she brought in interesting guest speakers. She was, of course, very intelligent and organized, but those were the least of her qualities. (Tiffany)

KEY IDEAS

✓ Students enjoy learning and remember more when they engage with content actively, according to their unique style, by moving, touching, illustrating, acting, building, debating, and on and on.

✓ Active learning is especially meaningful when it connects to students' real life outside the classroom.

✓ Primary resources flood classroom learning with authenticity and meaning.

✓ Cooperative learning means more than putting students into groups and hoping for the best. It is a way of classroom life that includes specific steps to ensure successful outcomes.

✓ Choices in what to study and how to demonstrate learning help students take control and ownership of their education.

8

High Expectations

■ I really can't say enough good things about her. She taught math with a passion. She was genuinely concerned about her students and their learning. She was kind and compassionate. At the same time, she worked us. There was no slacking off in her class. She pushed us hard enough that we struggled but not so hard that we failed. And if anyone began to fall behind, she'd work with the student after school, before school, during lunch or on weekends. I got a B in her class, and I worked hard to get it. (Bill)

PERSEVERANCE

Learning and striving for understanding and mastery requires concentrated and sustained effort. Although students constantly learn from daily experience, the targeted, systematic curriculum of schooling, when they might prefer more benign pursuits, demands focused perseverance, with no slacking off, in order to be successful.

Emperor penguins, living and breeding in the harsh climate of Antarctica, offer a compelling model of such focused perseverance. The film *March of the Penguins* (Jaquet 2005) dramatically documents how penguins abandon their ocean home and food source to walk long distances in search of a stable breeding area thick with ice. With unwavering determination to preserve their families, mother and father penguins alternate huddling with fellow penguins and their chicks for life-sustaining warmth in the frigid conditions.

As one penguin parent steadfastly cares for the newly hatched chick, the other short-legged, web-footed penguin slowly makes his way the seventy-mile distance back to open waters, persisting through harsh, subzero blizzards. Collectively, the penguins have a goal—eat their fill from the ocean depths and trek the seventy miles back to bring food for the baby penguins until they can survive on their own. Back and forth, emperor penguins persevere through forbidding conditions. With no slacking off, their success ensures the perpetuation of the species.

Feeling somewhat like the penguins, I faced penetrating blizzard conditions while teaching at the University of Minnesota. It was there that I learned something about perseverance from watching Derek, a resolute student, blind from birth. Although we never talked, I passed Derek regularly as he ventured across the large campus, always with a tenacious gait and a full backpack. He carried himself with an air of confidence that belied his lifetime challenges.

One bitterly cold winter day, the temperature dropped steadily to twenty-eight degrees below zero, and the wind chill felt much colder. Bundled in my long down coat and wool hat, I hurried across campus to escape the chill and happened to notice Derek. To keep warm, he had wrapped his entire head in a wool scarf, like a mummy.

The stark realization that he could, indeed, completely cover his eyes startled me into imagining what it must be like to pursue a degree through eyes that cannot see. In the weeks that followed, Derek's inner vision to complete an education reassured me that perseverance, despite the obstacles, is not only possible but also available for anyone.

How do students learn perseverance? Does it come from facing down life's obstacles in the way that Derek faced them? Does it come from an inborn sense of optimism or from attitudes that parents pass down to their children, attitudes that honor academic effort as a way to pave the long road to success? And what role do teachers play in influencing students to persevere with classroom curriculum year after year? How do teacher expectations come face-to-face with student resistance?

■ She's been the toughest teacher that I have had to date. At the time, I hated her. She always gave us ten- to fifteen-page analytical papers to do in three days, meaning that at least two of the nights, you had to stay up the whole night. Now that I look back, she gave me the most effective lessons on perseverance, planning, and logical thinking that I have ever had. Sloppy work was unacceptable; therefore, one had to try. I received a B+ in the class. I have never felt like I earned a grade so much in my life. Being a student under her made me proud to be an African American woman aspiring to teach, and thanks to her, I feel like there's no class in which I can't excel. (Mary)

Understandably for students, three days may be short notice for lengthy papers, and a discerning teacher knows when to raise the academic bar and when to reduce the academic workload. Be assured that in any school, students know which teachers are lax and which teachers hold high expectations. The dilemma for teachers is to find the appropriate balance and keep students on board.

A few years back, I had a conversation with a student teacher about the requirement to periodically observe other teachers throughout the high school and to journal his insights. Because he didn't know many of the teachers on staff and he wanted to visit classrooms taught by the best teacher examples, he decided to ask his students who he should observe to learn how effective teachers teach. His students consistently steered him to the teachers who challenged them, those who had high expectations for performance and required nothing less than students' best work. Students know the difference.

■ I played basketball for the sophomore team but was moved up to junior varsity at the end of our season. My junior varsity coach told me that I probably wouldn't get a lot of playing time, but wouldn't it be nice to play with the "big dogs," as he called them. I jumped at the chance. He was the life of the team, its energy and compassion. Don't get me wrong—he'd kick you in your butt if he thought you needed it. He later told me that if I worked as hard in the gym as I had been in his classes, I could play varsity basketball the next year. Again, it was the fact that I didn't want to let him down that made me strive to be better. He had a way of getting his players and students to do things for him and for themselves. I worked hard and made the varsity team my junior year. He never let me stop working, though; he was my most influential teacher ever. (John)

ABILITY EXPECTATIONS

If teachers simply demand good work from students, teachers might be met with anything from noncompliance to grudging or tepid cooperation. By far, students are more willing, even eager, to persevere in school when it is clear that someone believes in their ability to accomplish the work and be successful. And, as teachers can attest, the first and greatest influence on students' self-perception of ability comes from their parents. Teachers take up in school what parents began at home.

A prime example is Ben Carson, who grew up poor in inner-city Detroit, where his mother, a single parent with little education, cleaned houses to keep food on the table (Carson 2006). Young Ben, a devotee of lazy habits, consistently received the lowest grades in his class in every subject until his mother decisively decreed a change, maintaining that Ben was capable and that his only way out of poverty was a good education. Her high expectations included limiting Ben's television viewing to two approved programs a week.

She further insisted that Ben visit the library and choose two books to read each week with the expectation that he prepare written book reports for her on each book—all this in addition to his regular homework. Ben's mother summarily dismissed his futile protests. She consistently told Ben that he was smart, that he could be at the top of his class, and that he was going to college. Period.

Ben soon found that reading on a wide variety of topics helped him to better grasp his schoolwork, and the things he learned through books bred wider and deeper academic interests and pursuits. Subsequently, Ben rose to the top of his class, graduated from college and medical school, and at age thirty-three became the director of pediatric neurosurgery at Johns Hopkins University Hospital, where he made medical history by separating Siamese twins joined at the back of the head.

According to Dr. Ben Carson, the difference between poverty and success began with his mother's expectations but quickly spread to include his teachers' high expectations and their unwavering support throughout his academic journey. When students come to school with a foundation of high expectations already laid at home, teachers have a ready-made opportunity to build on those expectations, like taking an existing steel frame and building a skyscraper, shaping it toward increasing levels of self-sufficiency.

Ben's inspiring climb from at-risk student to respected physician begs the question of teacher expectations for students whose parents are disengaged, parents who provide little or no support at home. Should teachers give up on such students? No. I recall a teacher's response to a group of fellow teachers: "Remember, we are not teaching the parents, we are teaching the kids." We cannot change a student's parents, and students from unsupportive backgrounds will ever be in classrooms across the country in every school. They, too, deserve the best education has to offer.

Regardless of students' backgrounds, teachers who believe in hope and possibility can still make inroads and steer students academically. It requires love, commitment, and persistence. As a group, teachers are among the few influential adults who can venture into a quasi-parental role and fill the "I believe in you" gap, setting the steel frame mind-set for students otherwise deprived of high expectations.

■ When I had her for advanced placement (AP) English, the first thing she told us is that we were smart and could read anything if we put our minds to it. She said, "All of the literature we read in this class is in English, so expect to be able to understand it." With this mind frame, we dove into an array of books, essays, and poetry. If stressed, we went outside, lay in a field, and she did a relaxation exercise with us. Her confidence that we would get what we needed to get done made me feel at ease. When it came time to take the AP exam for college credit, she told us that college credit would be icing on the cake. The value of the class had already happened. (Kelly)

Students have uncanny insight into their teachers' perceptions of them as individual learners and achievers. They know if their teachers believe in them. Likewise, students understand when teachers do not really believe in them, and that message is mutely answered with "why try?" And, without the benefit of optimistic teacher expectations, students won't try unless they have strong overriding parental expectations for education or unless they somehow muster the internal determination to show others they can be successful anyway (Good and Nichols 2001). In truth, student performance is often a poignant self-fulfilling prophecy stemming from teacher, parent, and personal expectations.

An early classic study demonstrated the notion of self-fulfilling prophecy and the role of teacher expectations (Rosenthal and Jacobson 1968). Researchers administered an intellectual capacity test to students at an elementary school located in a low-socioeconomic neighborhood. Afterward, the researchers randomly chose 20 percent of the students and purposefully conveyed false predictions to their teachers, telling them that this particular student group had high intellectual capacities and could be expected to demonstrate high achievement during the school year. At the end of the school year, the students were retested, and the same 20 percent, labeled as high achievers, showed significantly higher improvement than did the 80 percent who were not labeled as intellectually talented.

It takes commitment on the part of teachers to avoid preconceived notions about students and avoid the personal prejudice that seduces teachers into lazy attitudes, hindering their ability to provide a quality education to all students. Teachers who find themselves plagued with creeping bias would do well to engage in honest self-inventory, trace personal prejudices to early sources of socialization, and resolve to challenge faulty beliefs at every turn (Ponterotto, Utsey, and Pedersen 2006).

High expectations are not generated by poring over student records to identify the able from the not so able, and holding high expectations is more than a rah-rah speech to energize students at the beginning of a school year. Students can discern predictable cheerleading attempts to bolster class performance. Instead, astute teachers mentor students as unique individuals, unpacking their extraordinary and diverse talents, and championing those abilities as harbingers of current progress and future success.

■ She pressed us to do the very best that we could and would not accept anything less. I remember that her major emphasis was teaching us how to write. In her opinion, when we first arrived in her classroom, none of us knew how to write—there was no way, she told us, that any college would put up with our writing. So she set out to turn us all into college-level writers. For a time, I had a problem with the low grades she gave me, so much so that, after several complaints to my mother, my mother set an appointment for us to talk about my grades. At the appointment, this teacher told me that she thought I was the best writer she had in any of her classes up to that point and that she was hard in grading me because she knew I would keep trying to do better. She hoped to help me become a better writer. Well,

I have become a better writer (though this brief paragraph is not a very good testament to this statement), and I even hope to become a professional writer. I have her to thank for this. (Brandon)

PATIENT PERSISTENCE

Pressing students to do their best, patient mentoring when students slip below expectations, and believing in students even when they don't yet believe in themselves is the demanding and draining yet rewarding work of teaching. It unfolded in just that way with me and my student, Victor, as he organized and wrote his master's thesis. Week after week, Victor trudged into my office and slumped into a chair, handing me his latest thesis revision. It was tough going for both of us.

In reality, Victor didn't need a master's degree at this time; he could get a teaching job with his current bachelor's degree and credential, and perhaps he considered quitting at times. I assured him that I believed in him, keeping the bright vision of his long-term goal ever before him. He wanted to be done and gone (doesn't everyone?), yet his thesis needed more substance, so I challenged his thinking and encouraged him to persevere with additional research, more articulate writing, and careful editing. It was touch-and-go most of the time.

Outwardly, Victor wore an expectant smile as we patiently powwowed over his work, but his confidence waned as he faced yet another revision. I continued to bolster his courage and press for excellence; neither could be ignored. In the end, Victor succeeded, graduated, and landed his dream teaching job at the school and grade level he most wanted. Not long afterward, he sent me a gift, a small book with his handwritten inscription, "Your thoughtful perseverance and professionalism inspired me to success. This book is small, but the title is you—*Because You Believed in Me.* Sincerest thanks . . ."

■ When you walked into her classroom, you knew she had high expectations for you. She encouraged me to have faith in myself and my writing ability. Before her class, I did not enjoy writing. Now, I love to write. She taught the importance of patience and revision when writing. She took each student to her desk individually to review their papers with them. She did this in a relaxed, positive way. She gave us constructive criticism about our paper, but she would also always compliment something in our paper as well. (Miranda)

Perseverance requires the patience to try again, to keep moving forward and not give up until the goal is in sight and within grasp. All things considered, many students find it difficult, if not impossible, to patiently endure and persevere in isolation from feedback and encouragement. They need a teacher who sets the bar appropriately high, and, with consistent support, students rise to all they can be when someone not only believes in them but also endures with them through thick and thin, regardless of how students might grumble and resist at the time.

■ My chemistry teacher was the teacher everyone hated, including me. It wasn't until college that I grew to appreciate and respect her. She accepted no excuse for less than our best. She had high expectations for every student. She continually put forth challenges for us. She demanded full cooperation and made sure we never failed. She patiently retaught material when needed and remained available for extra help. She was there to teach and prepare us for "real life" or college, whichever the case may be, not to be the "most popular teacher." (Jade)

Jade suggested that her teacher patiently retaught material and didn't allow students to fail. Curiously, the way that students think about their past failures is a powerful predictor of their future achievement. Teachers who explore the way students view their poor performance by questioning them can subsequently use the information to students' advantage without compromising high expectations.

For example, students who attribute their poor performance to a lack of ability are less motivated to try their best with subsequent schoolwork. For that reason, teachers play a crucial role in peeling back how students reason through their poor performance. When questioned, what do students say about substandard performance on a particular task? Not enough study time? Not enough interest? Not enough ability?

Teachers can positively impact students' motivation to persist and not give up when they challenge students to view their work in perspective, guiding them to attribute poor performance to the need for different study strategies or thinking processes rather than conceding to any student's focus on perceived lack of ability (Weiner 1986). Wise teachers suspend sorting students into able and unable categories and instead spend their time helping students revise faulty perceptions about their ability and patiently teaching students differentiated study and process strategies that work for their individual learning needs.

CHALLENGING MEDIOCRITY

■ He inspired me and my classmates by challenging us. He simply would not let us slide by. When a student prepared and did well in class, it felt good. More teachers should challenge their students and not accept mediocrity. (Daniel)

In an inner-city Chicago school district, Marva Collins challenged her students and would not accept mediocrity (Collins and Tamarkin 1990). The Marva Collins Preparatory School operates with the prevailing philosophy that all children can learn. From the beginning, Collins enrolled students considered learning disabled and at risk. She tackled the vital foundation, familiar to all teachers—get students to read well and to love it.

Teaching phonics rules with captivating chants, Collins systematically shaped more confident readers. She challenged students with a wide assortment of books, stockpiled from charity events and used bookstores. She intentionally chose books just a bit higher than her students' current reading level, and she recounted Theodore's surprise when she handed him *Moby Dick*, the thickest book on the shelf. Theodore protested that the book belonged to big kids because it had too many words and no pictures.

Collins reminded him that words were just made up of sounds, sounds they had mastered, and therefore he could read most if not all the words. Armed with that challenge, Theodore dug into the book, conquered the plot, and proudly carried his "thick book" everywhere, subsequently sharing his literary insights in a class report. Theodore and his classmates could not slide by with mediocrity, nor did they want to once they caught Collins's confidence in their ability.

Within a year, Collins's students improved their academic achievement five grade levels. She practiced her belief that all students can learn despite their background or previous achievement, and she made sure students knew they could learn so they would persevere through a demanding curriculum. The challenge to shun mediocrity is possible and essential at all grade levels—elementary school, middle school, high school, and college—as exemplified in the following student recollections.

Elementary School

■ One of the things I remember is her demanding "WWWs" which stood for Mrs. W's wonderful worksheets. These were challenging grammar exercises with original sentences she created using our classmates as the topic. The sentences increased in difficulty as the year progressed. One assignment had to be correct before moving on to the next. She taught for mastery. (Liz)

Middle School

■ She rarely relied on workbooks, so her classes were innovative and exciting—never monotonous. Her class was never easy, but because she was excited about the material, we all worked exceptionally hard. Middle school was a long time ago, but I remember field trips related to books we had read, and we wrote and presented constantly. (Allison)

High School

■ He connected to all levels of high school students. He challenged the high-ability students but allowed extra time for students who needed it. The first day of class, we filled out challenge cards. He kept those cards, and once a month we had an individual meeting to discuss the goals. He went out of his way to make the goals reachable. (Kendall)

College

■ He assigned a number of insightful and controversial readings in my college history course. Probably the best two things he contributed were his ability to challenge us with tough questions and a willingness to learn from student contributions. He used a number of recordings by historians to supplement his lectures, and he never replied to a difficult question without providing two points of view. (Kevin)

STANDARDS AND ACCOUNTABILITY

In an era of federal standards for student performance, holding high expectations is not just a good idea to try when convenient—it is mandated. Teachers themselves face dubious challenges as they grapple with how to integrate meaningful, creative activities with standards that demand increasing accountability for all students despite their background, first language, ethnicity, culture, interests, or ability.

An astute teacher's core philosophy of high expectations rises above mere adherence to mandated standards and accountability. For teachers driven by a fundamental belief in the best possible future for each student, high expectations become more authentic and personal—between teachers and their students. Teachers who embrace high expectations breed a broader vision for students than ticking a check-off list of standards that enable students to transition to the next grade, to exit high school, or to enroll in college.

This broader, more personal vision for student accountability played out for a student teacher who lamented her placement with the lowest-achieving English class in her assigned school, a function, she sighed, of being a student teacher with absolutely no clout. Being a high achiever herself, she determined not to let this opportunity slip by without galvanizing high expectations for this lackluster group.

Her teaching dilemma initially surfaced when her students simply would not engage in her repeated and valiant attempts to dialogue with them about a book, a classic novel they were reading at the time. For the discouraged student teacher, it was tempting to ride out the duration of her teaching assignment, doing the best she could to wrest a few modest comments from her listless students and to bequeath some predigested themes from the book.

Instead, to her credit, she took whatever time she needed to become acquainted with individual students, to awaken their dormant artistic and creative energy, and to hold them accountable for the content. She discovered that many of them liked to draw, design, and tinker around on computers.

Armed with new insights, she mobilized triad groups and designated them as literary agents assigned to design and sell the book. Each designer group chose a theme and created a multimedia presentation with graphics, sound, images, and written insights.

The student teacher refused to let students slide by with lazy sentences, mechanical errors, sloppy design, or faulty logic. High expectations ruled the classroom terrain. The day I visited, students fervently persevered, editing and polishing their multimedia designs and requesting feedback as they practiced their presentations, preparing for a wider, professional audience.

THE JOY OF LEARNING

If learning came easily, the burning satisfaction of mastering a concept or completing a task might remain an unkindled spark. The joy of learning comes from struggling with an idea or laboring through a task for a sustained time, persevering against the odds while brain neurons gradually connect in the necessary and synchronized way that learning requires. At the end of the struggle, like a flash of lightning in the dark recesses of the mind, the stunning discovery and clarity of a concept that before had seemed so puzzling and so dense is extraordinary.

Undeniably, human nature rails against the struggle and abhors the persistence that learning requires. Teachers are eminently positioned to defy human nature, press students with higher expectations than they might otherwise possess, and scaffold their efforts, laboring with them in the trenches while they battle toward success. Savvy teachers will not deprive students of the joy that comes from accomplishing more than they had dreamed for themselves.

■ I remember walking into English class my senior year of high school, the very first day and the very first hour. Of course, as a senior you're just about ready to get out and have fun. This teacher changed my entire attitude about many things! Hers was a pretty intense class that would take a lot of work and patience, but she made it so enjoyable that instead of dreading that class each morning, I honestly looked forward to going. (Andrea)

Jerome Bruner (1960), early founder of constructivism and believer in challenging students, encouraged teachers to inspire their students and press them to persevere through difficult material with the comment, "One of the least discussed ways of carrying a student through a hard unit of material is to challenge him with a chance to exercise his full powers, so that he may discover the pleasure of full and effective functioning. Good teachers know the power of this lure" (50).

KEY IDEAS

✓ Holding high expectations for students convinces them that their education matters.

✓ High expectations are effective when balanced with knowing when to press and when to back off.

✓ Helping students attribute poor performance to a need for different study strategies rather than a lack of ability or effort preserves their self-efficacy.

✓ Refusing to accept mediocrity must be accompanied by a message of support and belief.

✓ Believing in students, even in the face of little or no family support, and digging in the learning trenches with them can yield untapped nuggets of golden abilities.

9

Assessment

■ Before our first test, she began singing "Old MacDonald Had a Farm." We did five animals, and then she counted us off in our chairs, one to five, and matched the numbers with the five animals. We then had to make our assigned animal sounds to find our groups. Once in our groups, we took the test as a group. I thought this would be a bad experience; however, I found the group fighting for the answers they believed in and the other members of the group making them defend their positions. Then, before our final test, she brought a wand, a magic wand, and blessed us each on the head. (Jean)

THE UPSIDE TO TESTING
Many students rightfully view test taking as a real drag, an unwelcome interruption to an otherwise routine school day. And if the test is schoolwide and high stakes, the interruption is pronounced and elevated in significance to a ritual of mandatory attendance, number two pencils, and precise directives. Many students relate to anxious feelings that run the gamut from mild butterflies to damp palms to abject fear before submitting to a test. But Jean's teacher makes assessment seem tolerable—almost fun. Is it possible? All things considered, who wouldn't want to be blessed with a magic wand if it could help? And some might willingly squawk animal sounds to stimulate thinking. Can teachers transform test anxiety from a mental vise grip to a curious cognitive adventure?

■ A specific example that comes to mind was his way of making students keep up with current events. He made the game "Jeopardy" into a current events game. We got extra credit for answering questions for ourselves and as a whole for the team. The following week we had a quiz on the game questions, and we were prepared. (Joseph)

I observed a creative teacher whose ebullient personality bubbled close to the surface, spilling over in broad smiles and hearty laughter. I visited his classroom on test preparation day as he handily engaged students in a chemistry relay race. Lined in rows, students joined the friendly competition as if hoping to win the assessment lottery with the correct combination of chemical letters and numbers.

The relay began when the first students in each row ran to a large brown box to retrieve questions, and the activity continued as they fanned out to write answers on the whiteboard. An uncertain answer cued the second student in a row to race to the board with a team-generated revision. Before picking a new question from the box, students deposited previous questions in one of three bowls labeled "easy," "average," or "hard" to designate their opinion of a question's difficulty. As the relay wound down, the teacher reviewed questions in the "difficult" bowl, expressing confidence in his students' ability to "learn the material cold," as he would say. In the realm of test preparation, fraught with anxiety and uncertainty, this memorable class hummed with brainpower.

■ One of the fun things she did took place before a test; we had a quiz contest over the material. We had fun competing in teams while reviewing the material. It always helped me do better. I have had many wonderful teachers through my education. So many, it was hard to pick, but this one teacher was outstanding in my book. (Margaret)

HOMEWORK WARS

Before administering tests, teachers regularly assess student progress along the way with projects, papers, and myriad other homework assignments. Beyond question, homework is a lightning rod for students, parents, and teachers. Backpacks laden with homework can burden the most conscientious learner, and frustrated parents chafe under the responsibility of monitoring one or more children through this nightly ritual that cuts deeply into family time.

Teachers typically assign too much homework. Studies with thousands of students demonstrate a minimal relationship between homework and academic achievement for elementary children (Cooper 2007), but a very limited amount of homework (no more than ten minute increments per grade level) can help elementary students develop regular study habits.

The relationship between homework and academic achievement grows stronger when students reach high school, but teachers in one subject area would do well to keep in mind that homework is also assigned by teachers in other subject areas. In the end, students hope that teachers will not make homework a contest of who can assign the most but instead consider reasonable and efficient ways to determine what students have learned.

■ She wanted us to leave her classes knowing that we had learned something, but she realized that different students are more comfortable with different types of assessments, so she included them all. She assigned creative homework projects and oral reports as well. (Angela)

If compelled to assign homework, the most creative teachers engage students, from time to time, with congenial real-life homework assignments that appeal to the whole family, activities that draw the family together without wasting their valuable time. In this way, families can spend a few minutes exploring a topic rather than battling through another long and stressful evening (Balli, Demo, and Wedman 1998).

For example, my cell phone rang one afternoon, and I heard a small, sweet voice. Our granddaughter and first grader, Casey, called to ask me a few questions for math homework. Did she want help with a computation worksheet? No, nothing that mundane. Adopting an uncharacteristically grown-up voice, Casey proceeded to ask me how much a candy bar cost when I was a little girl; she further inquired how much a stamp cost and how much gasoline cost.

I entertained her with stories, amazing her when I bragged how I could buy a very large Hershey candy bar for a nickel when I was a little girl a long, long time ago. "Why do you want to know?" I queried. She explained, in first-grade terms, how she compared today's prices, which her teacher provided, with prices for the same items when Grandma grew up.

A few weeks later, my cell phone rang again. "We are doing a graph in school. How many pets do you have?" Again, it was Casey, our budding first-grade mathematician and analyst. Her teacher could have assigned a worksheet to assess Casey's knowledge of numbers and basic comparisons, and Casey likely completed plenty of them, but her teacher also developed more imaginative ways to assess understanding, and in so doing she brought generations together and gave Casey, her classmates, and families an authentic and enjoyable way to connect over homework.

TIGER SKIN ASSESSMENT

■ The part I liked best was how the assessment methods varied—we were tested, wrote poetry, wrote papers, constructed projects, and did group presentations. For each unit, groups of students chose a topic and presented it to the rest of the class. The teacher allowed us a great deal of flexibility—sometimes we wrote commercials or presented a play including costumes. We loved it even though it was by far the most difficult class at our school. (Lindsey)

Lindsey's recollection conveys the importance of assessing student performance in more than one way. A narrow, single-focused assessment can actually give a misleading picture of students, similar to what happened when a mother tiger examined what she thought were her cubs. The true story unfolded in a California zoo where a tiger gave birth, prematurely, to a set of triplet tiger cubs that died soon after birth.

When the mother tiger became despondent, zoo veterinarians determined that she might improve with a replacement set of tiger cubs. The vets could locate only three baby piglets, but taking a chance, they wrapped each piglet in a tiger skin and introduced them to the mother tiger. Based on a surface-level assessment, their furry tiger skin, the mother took the babies as her own. Although this unusual case worked out for the mother tiger, whose health improved, she was notably fooled by a single assessment that gave an inaccurate picture of her replacement cubs. The mother tiger explored no further than one dimension.

Growing up through a lockstep school system, we have been reared on an assessment diet of standardized tests; therefore, as adults, we are conditioned to measuring achievement based primarily on paper-and-pencil performance. Such tests offer just one dimension of a student's knowledge, generally less than valid, like piglets in a tiger's skin.

Looking back on my own childhood, I recall my parents emerging from a parent–teacher conference with a single pronouncement that summed up my academic self with numbers reflecting my scores on standardized achievement tests. The scores pinpointed my standing among students nationally, from top to bottom, like tiger piglets lined up from strongest to weakest. This one-dimensional pronouncement offered a skewed picture of my overall abilities, like peering into a distorted mirror at an amusement park and trying to see the real me. The same can be said for students everywhere.

The system still compels administrators to respond actively to standardized test scores, so much so that it remains a topic at many staff meetings. And thus, teachers are required to administer "benchmark assessments" throughout the school year and focus on the "low" areas of student progress. While attending to areas of lower progress has merit, testing can become burdensome, interfering with the natural flow of learning in the classroom. So what is a teacher to do?

Fortunately, since my school days, many creative teachers have moved beyond myopic measurements of academic achievement. Although school districts and the federal government continue to mandate specific standardized tests, wise teachers develop multifaceted assessments that uncover and celebrate numerous ways for students to demonstrate their learning.

Now, when parents attend parent–teacher conferences, teachers and students can display portfolios, writing samples, individual projects, drawings, and student-designed multimedia, with test results making up only one of many perspectives on student progress. Indeed, teachers and policymakers generally agree that judgments and decisions about students and their academic achievement should never be made on the basis of a single assessment (Popham 2007).

■ She was good at teaching in a way that made me remember. She didn't just give us tests. She allowed us to be evaluated by writing papers, including our own ideas, and by reading and critiquing books. I think that it is important not to stress testing so much. Many students are not able to do well on tests, yet they are very intelligent. (Tatiana)

Although I believe in multiple ways to assess student progress, I confess that it too often manifests itself in theory rather than consistent practice.

Several years ago, I embarked on a grand experiment in order to break out of the constraining assessment box lined with dreary paper-and-pencil tests. At the time, I taught educational psychology, a core curriculum requirement for all teacher education students. The course included concepts relevant to their future classroom teaching practice, one of which is assessment.

I had regularly and meticulously taught multiple assessment strategies, including performance assessments, tangible products, portfolios, journals, and drawings. When it came time for the midterm and final exams, however, I habitually reverted to a traditional essay test. Students who could write effectively did well on these tests, while other students, less verbally inclined, struggled to clearly express their understanding in writing.

To better practice what I preached, I decided to offer students alternate ways to demonstrate their knowledge. A good share of students welcomed the opportunity and carefully proposed unique alternate exams. Some students composed songs with each verse covering an array of concepts, some developed multimedia presentations highlighted with sound and visuals, others interviewed practitioners probing with relevant questions, several designed intriguing experiments to investigate core concepts, and a few developed extensive scripts complete with action, music, and costuming. The students surprised me, inspired me, and taught each other in ways I could not have predicted.

RUBRIC ASSESSMENT

Although assessing student learning in multiple ways through projects and performances is more creative and authentic than a steady diet of paper-and-pencil tests, the time needed for adequately assessing projects can drive even the most efficient teachers to revert back to scanning basic multiple-choice and true-or-false questions. To counter the temptation toward single-minded objective assessments, teachers can use rubrics. In this way, students know evaluation criteria in advance, and teachers know how to consistently apply evaluation standards to subjective assignments.

A rubric is a systematic assessment tool that includes a rating system and criteria for the assignment (Kronowitz 2008). Each criterion in a rubric is accompanied by a range of performance indicators. The more specific the performance indicators, the more information students have about expectations for a particular assignment.

For example, I created the following basic rubric for an essay paper, and I distribute variations on this rubric at the time I assign the essay. It helps students complete the assignment according to my expectations. As students become accustomed to rubrics as an assessment tool, teachers often enlist student participation in creating rubrics, thus increasing the chances that students will take ownership of the assignment and expectations (see table 9.1).

Using a grade level–appropriate rubric not only helps students know what is expected but also helps in evaluating the assignment. For example, I read an essay, circle the appropriate performance indicator in each row, include specific comments throughout the paper, and write general comments on the rubric. Finally, I assign points on a continuum for each performance indicator. Even if an assignment is challenging, students understand how to approach it.

If students have questions about their grade, we can conference based on performance indicators such as "logical," "clear," "concrete," or "accurate." For performance indicator headings that invite improvement, I use words such as "strengthen proficiency," which offers an opening for continued progress, rather than counterproductive words such as "poor" or "unacceptable," which dampens motivation. The first time I assign and evaluate a paper, I conference with students and allow them to revise if they wish to improve their work.

Table 9.1. Sample Scoring Rubric for Essay

Criteria	High Proficiency	Proficiency	Strengthen Proficiency
Major claim	Precise and well-developed major claim	Generally clear major claim	Vague major claim loosely connected to topic
Evidence and rationale	Concrete, detailed evidence to support major claim	Good but less thorough evidence for major claim	Irrelevant or incomplete evidence for major claim
Coherence and clarity	Sequence of ideas is clear, logical, and organized	Generally clear ideas less effectively organized	Less clarity, challenging for reader to follow
Mechanics	Accurate spelling and grammar throughout	Generally accurate spelling and grammar with few errors	Mechanics need attention
Teacher comments			

The more challenging the assignment, the more students benefit from the performance indicators that rubrics and conferencing provide. For busy teachers, the Internet has a free and incredible rubric building website that offers criteria choices for a wide assortment of assessments, including those for math, science, writing, speaking, art, music, group projects, and multimedia, to name but a few. The website address is http://rubistar.4teachers.org.

Whether or not the assessment is a project, performance, or test and whether or not the assessment includes a rubric, when teachers offer specific feedback, it dismantles the evaluation puzzle and elevates assessment to an active, progressive learning process that encourages students to think and grow.

■ It was not uncommon for my high school to scatter "smart people" to every Ivy League school in the nation, and they all took AP [advanced placement] American history with Mr. G. He was like a "god," some sort of entity that I looked up to. After I failed my second exam, he called me into his office and told me that I wasn't taking his class very seriously. He was right—I wasn't. I was petrified by this conversation, but he specifically pointed out what I was doing wrong and showed me how to improve. He taught me to think. (Diana)

TIMELY FEEDBACK

"You assigned it, you grade it," my students often needle me with wry smiles as they pile papers, journals, projects, and notebooks on my desk. They make a good point. If students go to the work of grinding out complex assignments, the least I can do is be respectful enough to read their work in a timely manner. The key is to review and assess student work while the content is still relevant in their minds and to offer specific feedback that confirms and challenges their thinking. Actually getting to the reading, evaluating, and specific feedback is another matter. Teachers procrastinate too.

■ She pushed herself and us. She rarely kept an assignment longer than a day, and we got it back the next day. She often gave comments on cassette tapes so she could fully explain and verbally compliment each piece without taking time out of the classroom. (Brooke)

To fight the temptation to procrastinate, I deliberately wrap assessment work with a sense of relaxation. An oxymoron, work and relaxation mean different things to different teachers. For me, relaxed work means grading papers at home, sitting in a large easy chair with my feet up near a lighted fireplace, or lounging on the backyard patio. With soft background music, I address the stack of papers beside me. I focus on each student as an interesting individual and imagine him or her sitting across from me. I probe what I can learn, inspired by my students' efforts to apply course concepts.

I keep a rainbow of pens for writing comments but avoid red pens after chagrined students grimaced when I "bled" on their work. I attach a completed rubric to the back of the paper so that the feedback is private. Typically, my summary comments follow a sandwich technique, starting with something I liked about the paper (bread), followed by something for the student to work on (meat), and concluding with words of encouragement for future progress (bread).

■ Instead of just putting a grade on our paper and telling us what we did wrong, this teacher found something positive about what we had written. If I did have some mistakes on my paper, he would say, "Instead of writing like this, why don't you do this." He wrote specific comments. He didn't just say, "You're right," or "You're wrong"; he told us what was right or what we needed to improve, along with specific suggestions. This is a sign of a great teacher. (Gabrielle)

IS THIS ON THE TEST?

"Will this stuff be on the test?" is a familiar line that students toss at teachers on a regular basis. Some students find it all but impossible to separate essential from nonessential content on their own. Can any academic endeavor be more disheartening for students than to encounter a test only to discover that the questions therein cover content obscured somewhere deep in the course? As luck would have it, students might have thoroughly chewed and digested every content morsel, ready to spit it back, but alas, what they studied is nowhere on the test that stares menacingly back at them. Fair and honest teacher practice explicitly links instruction to assessment (Guillaume 2008).

■ We knew exactly what we were expected to learn. Her objectives were clear. I do not like teachers who are vague (i.e., "You'll need to know some information from chapter 6."). It causes students to know a

little about a lot of material. I remember things easier if I understand
what I need to know with a study guide. (Natalie)

Naturally, teachers can assess only a small sample of what they teach or
what they hope students will learn, but in the face of an upcoming test,
students appreciate it when teachers provide a study guide, not one that un-
ethically details specific test questions but one that comprises important concepts and a sampling of the types of questions a teacher could ask.

■ She was known as the handout queen. Everything she wanted us to
know she put in a handout. She further made it evident what information would need to be recalled at test time. Throughout readings
and lectures, she emphasized important points in humorous ways.
She would say, "As I'm reading the characteristics of the heroic
metatype to you, I will clear my throat when I come to a possible test
question." She proceeded to do this very dramatically. (Patricia)

For students, the first test in a school year or the first test from a new
teacher is often an intimidating venture into the unknown. To counteract my
students' uncertainty, I began to administer a sample test at the beginning of
the school year to cue them about what to expect. Students enjoy making informed guesses on the sample test where it won't count, and in the ensuing
discussion, their informed guessing alerts me to their prior content knowledge and reminds me to preassess their understanding about upcoming topics as well.

■ One of her most positive traits was her testing strategies. Before she
gave us the test, she gave us the objectives that the test would cover
and also what level of thinking the questions would be, for example,
one knowledge question and two application questions. I thought
she was a fair teacher. If you came to class and did your work, then
you got a good grade. (Melanie)

DEALING WITH DEADLINES

When assigning projects and homework, teachers often include a submission
deadline so that they can assess student understanding before moving on to

new material. Most students admit that meeting assignment deadlines is at best annoying and at worst formidable. Adhering to deadlines, meeting a problem or difficult task head-on, requires a mental discipline that many people try to avoid (Peck 1978).

Predictably, students with good intentions but weak mental discipline procrastinate, hoping that deadlines will dissolve (I once had an English major tell me that he would rather clean toilets than write an essay). Over time, the dreaded deadline stalks procrastinators like a stealthy cheetah, gathering speed as it approaches, until the procrastinator can no longer hide. Consequently, the procrastinator either pleads for an extension, pulls an all-nighter, or lets the deadline pass without submitting the work.

■ In middle school, things could sometimes be very unfair. Not in her class. She was fair to all of her students and made every opportunity equal. She was a strict teacher, but because she was strict about on-time assignments and conduct, you really learned. I learned more that year than any other year. (Kristen)

As a teacher, I used to be a real softy when it came to deadlines until I learned a dire lesson. Many of my students regularly ignored established deadlines knowing that I would give them an extension with little or no penalty. And so, the late work would come, intermittently and unpredictably, plaguing me like a winter cough.

During one grading term, adherence to assignment deadlines dwindled to the point that over half my students submitted a substantial amount of work four days after the final exam and two days before graduation. I knew things had to change. I reasoned that the discipline of deadlines would not only preserve my sanity but also strengthen student responsibility, a worthy and necessary life skill.

So, I contacted the dillydallying students for an informal conference to investigate the extent to which they submitted late work to every teacher. With sheepish temerity, they admitted to knowing which teachers accepted late work and which did not. They agreed that I should adopt a stricter policy. I did. Now students submit assignments and projects on the due date in order to receive credit. I allow one class period of grace for unavoidable life circumstances—a remnant of the softy left in me.

■ This class did have deadlines and grades, and we were taught that no one would be standing over us in life reminding us of that, and therefore it was not the teacher's job either. Along with freedom, we got responsibility. Through this teacher, I learned about teaching myself in all realms of life. (Sierra)

ASSESSING WITH EQUITY

The broad purpose of assessment is not to label students with deficiencies. On the contrary, all students deserve a fair opportunity to succeed, which means expending early effort to ensure that a student's background, language acquisition, learning differences, and special needs will not hinder academic progress. The wide arms of equitable assessment are intended to gather students in rather than to shut them out.

As such, assessment becomes what it is meant to be: a way to determine current progress from multiple perspectives with the goal of guiding students toward making continued progress using whatever avenue can support them. Early assessments can address underlying developmental or academic needs so that every student has a fair and equal opportunity to reach his or her potential.

■ I worked for her and graded papers. She explained how she planned her lessons and what she felt was important for all students to learn. She was a fair person. She gave every student an equal opportunity, which I can see now was very crucial to their academic careers. (Mikayla)

The priceless value of early assessment arrived up close and personal when our grandson, Jack, was born with a moderate hearing impairment, and he began to wear tiny hearing aids at three months old. The local school district admirably offered the services of two developmental specialists who interacted with six-month-old Jack and answered his parents' questions. On this and subsequent visits, specialists identified and assessed Jack's auditory needs and shored up support for his steady progress during his first few years to prepare him for school.

The district specialists offered Jack's parents a menu of strategies for helping him learn to talk, pronounce words, and detect what others say. The early assessment ensured equal opportunity for Jack, and now, at five years old, he talks as well as any child his age. A keen observer, he learned to tune in and grasp most conversations even without his hearing aids.

In fact, when Jack was three, I drove him to the beach, and because we planned to swim, Jack removed his hearing aids and gave them to me. During our ride to the beach, Jack kept up a running conversation from the backseat, and I answered each of his questions rather loudly, in my teacher voice, to ensure that he could hear me. Before long, he assured me that I did not have to talk loudly because "I can hear you far away Grandma." From the moment of his initial assessment, Jack had and, it is hoped, will continue to have fair and equal opportunities to succeed.

Likewise highlighting early assessment, Debbie Phelps, a middle school principal and mother of Olympic champion Michael Phelps, recounted Michael's diagnosis of attention deficit/hyperactivity disorder at age nine. Told that Michael would have trouble focusing on anything, Debbie encouraged and supported Michael's interest in swimming to help him focus on something he enjoyed. Debbie reported that pinpointing Michael's needs early, along with the routine swimming regimen and a great deal of patience, helped catapult Michael's life beyond what they could have predicted. Fair and timely assessments afford teacher and parent partners the information needed to pursue the equal opportunities that all children deserve.

TEACHERS AS COACHES

In the realm of assessment, a discerning teacher is like a coach evaluating every play. The goal is not to define deficiencies and remain stuck but rather to appraise the current situation and signal the next student play. For teachers, signaling the next play could mean organizing learning games to review content, providing study guides to illuminate concepts, setting deadlines to hold students responsible, creating rubrics to guide work, offering multiple ways for students to demonstrate progress, and giving specific feedback to encourage growth.

In classrooms built on community, teachers find ways to assess equitably and continuously, including not just formal assessments and projects but also the day-to-day informal observations that teacher coaches use to monitor progress and mentor students without the need for unending grade book markings.

Students are not the only ones who benefit from appropriate assessment and coaching. Teachers know that effective student assessment springs from ongoing and careful teacher self-assessment. Teachers who grow professionally plan opportunities to reflect on and assess their own practice—considering how teaching and learning is working in their classroom community.

■ The transition from elementary to middle school is a difficult one for many students. You go from a classroom with one teacher who really cares about you to a day filled with seven different teachers. None of those teachers gets to know you that well. My eighth-grade English teacher was an exception. A lot of teachers will teach their subject, and if you pay attention, you will do well, and if you don't, you will do poorly. Your grades reflect your effort. To this teacher, grades not only reflected the students' efforts but her efforts as well. If a student got an F, she believed she wasn't doing her job. Students rarely got Fs in her class. (Kelsey)

I admire teachers who find ways to join their students in the classroom learning community by becoming a student with them, regularly assessing not only their students' growth but their own growth as well, lest they become stagnant and burned out. A colleague once told me that he consistently appoints one evening a week for self-assessment on the previous week. He also reads an array of books and journal articles on educational topics that interest him to bridge the gaps in his thinking and practice.

Teachers do well to assess their work and continue to grow professionally and not because an administrator distributes articles, mandates continuing education, or schedules an in-service workshop. While these may be useful, teacher self-assessment is more personal, and teachers who target their own learning needs understand that personal growth is a lifelong process that pays big dividends in the classroom.

KEY IDEAS

✓ Figuring out ways to lace assessment with lighthearted preparation groups and games removes some of the anxiety and dread from evaluation.

✓ Effective assessment encompasses more than paper-and-pencil tests to include meaningful projects, demonstrations, products, and the like.

✓ Supporting students in assessment preparation with an appropriate study guide helps students retrieve and organize buried concepts and avoid surprises.

✓ Students deserve equitable and unbiased opportunities to learn, think, and demonstrate their knowledge.

✓ Assessment extends to teacher self-assessment and reflection about their professional growth.

III

BUILDING AUTHENTICITY

Now and then, as for this book, we reflect on the excellent teachers we have known, and at times it might be tempting to imitate those exemplary teachers. Analyzing the qualities and skills of such teachers, we speculate that if we were more knowledgeable, humorous, relaxed, scholarly, rigorous, articulate, creative, or a host of other admirable characteristics, then we might blithely and with finality brand ourselves excellent teachers—truly, an unproductive exercise.

Consider the perfect design and symmetry of snowflakes—complex, with no two alike, singular, distinctive, and incomparable—unique masterpieces of nature's handiwork. Ponder that vision in the context of teachers and teaching, and therein lies an important lesson: while it is worthy to gather useful ideas and strategies from a variety of great teachers, it is essential to be true to oneself, personally authentic, growing in character, competency, experience, and understanding over time.

Quite simply, each person who chooses to become a teacher and remain a teacher has a great deal to offer—unique gifts, background, personality, knowledge, and an immense capacity for making a difference in the classroom and in the lives of students. Ultimately, the goal is to be the best teachers we were meant to be, differing from other teachers but decidedly effective in our own way, with our own unmatched dynamic twist on teaching and learning.

10

Teaching Styles

■ This teacher was the most fun and surprising teacher I have ever had. We had been studying different views of psychology, and on the day we were to study B. F. Skinner and behaviorism, our teacher came running into the auditorium wearing a half mask and a curly red clown wig. We didn't know who it was at first! She spent the entire period talking in a foreign accent and calling herself "Boris Skinner" as if she were Skinner's long-lost relative. To demonstrate Skinner's stimulus-response theory, she had a huge bowl of Halloween candy, and every time someone answered a question, she threw handfuls of candy at them. I know none of us will ever forget B. F. Skinner's theory. (Hope)

ATTENTION AND ANTICS
In the frenzy of diversions that fuel the imagination and vie for student attention, a teacher's role—to spark interest in mathematics, reading, history, and science—is daunting at best. Although luring student attention from a myriad of distractions is challenging, good teachers strive for unique ways to make it happen. Securing student attention is not just a good idea; it is also essential to learning. Indeed, attention to the topic at hand is the starting gate for mental processing. The more focused the attention, the deeper the processing and the more that is retained (Atkinson and Shiffrin 1968; Craik and Lockhart 1972).

Teachers have long pursued and stockpiled attention-getting strategies. To catch and hold student attention, clever teachers muster a variety of tools, even outrageous ones, like the curly red clown wig. I know a middle school teacher who also dressed up in a crazy wig but added an outrageous shirt that had numbers written all over it. He was posing as an "irrational number." Such techniques are not just gimmicks; rather, they facilitate memory.

I'll admit that I seriously considered wearing a curly red clown wig for the next time I taught behaviorist theory and pictured myself donning a wig over my perfectly coifed hair, dissolving into laughter, and yanking the thing off. For me, it felt unnatural and goofy. Still, I appreciate teachers, like the following two, who are amazingly adept at costuming, completely unafraid to take self-deprecating risks.

■ To get some of his points across, my chemistry teacher would not be afraid to stand on his head, jump on his desk, and dress up. Some of his costumes included the atom, carbon molecules, and just goofy outfits to hold our attention. I want to be "crazy" like him. (Valerie)

■ She was as flexible as the subjects she brought up in class. Her approach to learning included her dressing up as a flower child to bring home the social influences of the 1960s on the nation—she had the class take sides and participate in several protest marches and mock sit-ins. (Erica)

HUMOR

While dressing up in content-related outfits is a guaranteed way for teachers to grab student attention and evoke reactions, other creative teachers hook students with their natural and well-planned humor, even without a costume trunk.

Well-placed classroom humor differs from simply telling jokes. Rather, classroom humor is aimed at putting a positive, amusing spin on the lesson content, inviting students to pause, reflect, and process concepts connected with playful laughter. Humor creates a congenial and relaxed classroom atmosphere. More important, cleverly crafted humor facilitates student retention across all grade levels to a greater extent than does the same lesson without added humor (Garner 2005; Pollak and Freda 1997).

■ The greatest quality he possessed was a sense of humor. You had to do the reading the night before to understand his jokes in class. When things started getting dull, he came up with a delightful anecdote about history. He supplemented our books with stories and trivia. Students realized that studying history could be fun and history itself had funny moments. (Tyler)

When planning humorous additions to lesson content, it is wise to consider the extent of its appeal to a particular student audience. For example, I recall the time I projected a *Far Side* cartoon on the classroom overhead. The cartoon directly related to the lesson in a funny offbeat way, and I chuckled in lighthearted glee while scanning the classroom to revel in the expected student response. I was met with blank stares and puzzled expressions. The students didn't get it.

Of course, *Far Side* cartoons can challenge the most discerning humorist, and in this case, the cartoon depicted regional country humor of bygone days and clearly did not connect to anything related to the lives of my diverse urban students. To salvage the teachable moment, I haplessly tried to explain the meaning behind the cartoon, and, ever so slowly, we enjoyed a spirited round of increasing chuckles. I learned the first lesson in using humor: know your audience and connect the humor to their background, interests, age, and culture.

■ She was funny with the dry, sarcastic sense of humor we were all trying to develop as middle school kids. I remember when she treated us to a home-made video on prepositions. She made this little squirrel as the main character. Everyone in class, including her, was in tears laughing because the poor thing was so disproportioned. I think by the end of the film we decided it looked more like a moose than a squirrel. The point is that she made the video herself and we all learned from it and enjoyed the learning process. (Danielle)

PROPS AND THEATRICS

In addition to humor and costuming, inventive teachers galvanize student attention with props, energizing students with tangible exhibits to illustrate a concept. Certainly, any concept can be outlined in a basic handout, a prop of sorts, but handouts, although useful, can be bland when used in isolation. Objects, on the other hand, make concepts memorable by enlisting the senses in blending verbal explanations with concrete images.

■ On the first day of class he introduced us to the basic elements of geography—latitude, longitude, and so on. He took an apple out of his pocket and started to peel it with a Swiss army knife. As he worked with the apple, he discussed the shape of the earth (round) and its crust (like the peel). He sliced the apple and asked questions aloud. All of us were shy and quiet because it was the first day of class in the big middle school. I tentatively raised my hand and answered his question, "Latitude?" "Right," he said, and handed me the first apple slice. I felt really smart that day. (Ava)

I observed a resourceful teacher use props to his teaching advantage when he brought a brown paper bag to class each day, set it furtively on the podium, and stared at it without saying a word. His students congregated around the bag before each class but were admonished not to touch or lift it. Curiosity overwhelmed the group as they implored the teacher to reveal the contents of the mysterious package. A daily guessing game ensued with intermittent teacher clues and increasing student enthusiasm. When a student conclusively unmasked the teacher's secret, he gingerly opened the bag, removed the hidden object of the day, and proceeded to connect the object with the day's lesson.

The brown paper bag and its mysterious contents convey the essence of an *anticipatory set* (Hunter 1982), an introductory agent, like props, humor, or theatrics, designed to build anticipation for what comes next. By cleverly building anticipation, teachers effectively unhook students from the tentacles of distractions, like reeling in fish from seaweed. The key is to invite students to the deck of the classroom and get them excited to be there. Versatile teachers sport a variety of anticipatory bait, from subtle and simple, like the brown bag, to startling and dramatic.

■ There was no such thing as a dull or boring class. At one point he even set up an entire situation to model what "stress" was like. He came in with an angry attitude and told us we were going to have a pop quiz, even though he had said we would never have one of those.

He then accused a student of cheating (the student was planted), and this student and the teacher got in a huge shouting match over it. We were also under time pressure to finish the quiz. The student left, screaming all the way. The teacher then did the same thing with a planted female student. She even slapped him when he accused her. She too left. We were then told we had a minute left. He eventually broke it off and described his intentions. The students loved it. (Nathan)

HEARTFELT GREETINGS

For teachers who feel out of their element or overwhelmed with the notion of dressing up, telling jokes, or using props, a simple but still powerful way to connect with students and invite their attention is to begin class with a gracious, heartfelt greeting and a few minutes of warm, congenial small talk. This seems patently obvious, but in the press of getting students settled and class started, the opportunity for a proper and sincere greeting can easily slip away.

I visited two middle school classrooms where the teachers practiced distinctly different greeting styles. I liked one but not the other. The first teacher stood at his classroom door every day to greet students with a smile and a hello, shaking their hands and tousling some heads. Even I could not resist as I scurried in line for his cordial and unexpected reception to the classroom. Once inside, students routinely greeted each other as part of this friendly learning community. Students loved it and proceeded to follow where the teacher led, not only through the classroom door but throughout the ensuing lesson as well.

Meanwhile, in the other classroom, the busy teacher remained glued to his desk, his head buried in the text, understandably consumed with a final check of the upcoming lesson. After visiting the first class, my antennae were alert for a welcome, but as students entered and settled into their seats, the teacher's head bobbed up belatedly with his first words, "Turn to page 55, and get out last night's homework." I missed the heartfelt welcome offered by the first teacher, and my attention drifted considerably throughout this more stifled class period.

As an elementary school board member, I once participated in a jubilant greeting ceremony to welcome students on the first day of classes. Faculty, administration, and board members each received a balloon bouquet or a sign that read "Welcome to School." As a group, we lined the sidewalks and streets to greet students as they arrived on the first day. Both younger and older students came to expect this yearly ritual, responding with grins, high fives, and waves as we shouted our greetings and shook hands—an incredible way to begin school and enlist student cooperation from day one.

The strong connection between teacher greeting styles and student attention is not unlike my encounters with a tiny but expressive hummingbird. Whenever I have a chance, I like to sit in our backyard and enjoy the natural beauty of a canyon that rims the back fence. Often, a green and violet iridescent hummingbird visits and intrigues me with his warm, sociable greeting.

Before making the rounds to each flower and the more serious task at hand, the bird hovers close to me, within two feet, at eye level, and with tiny wings fluttering in rapid blur, he pauses to notice me for several seconds. With quick movement, backward, forward, and vertical, the hummingbird returns again and again to meet with me before darting off to visit the nearby flowers. Offered willingly, with no expectations, the miniature feathered greeter welcomes me to the backyard and rivets my attention to what would otherwise be only passing notice of his nectar-gathering nature lesson.

Human nature craves welcome and appreciation. So whether teachers choose to dress up, use props, shake hands, or simply say, "Hello and welcome to class," teachers who delight in students as they spill into class find that by dividing joy among their students, their own joy multiplies.

■ When I was younger I was one of those students who did not want to leave my mom to come to school. Every day, my kindergarten teacher knew I was sad, and I would sit on her lap in the morning before school started. She made me feel welcome and loved. (Ashley)

PASSION AND PRESENCE

When teaching is done well, it is not a mechanical skill. Teachers can prepare perfectly organized lessons with diverse learning activities. Teachers can dress professionally, attain advanced degrees, and design attractive classrooms. As important as these things are, they are not enough. Excellent teaching is still an individual art with no two teaching styles alike in every respect. There is something about a unique artisan teacher who draws students in. Performers call it stage presence. It involves the essence of who teachers are: the way they carry themselves and their enthusiasm, passion, sense of purpose, and confidence.

■ What was her secret? It certainly wasn't physical presence or charisma. She was a tiny, wrinkled lady with white hair and horn-rimmed glasses. Her voice could be harsh and masculine, but when she began to tell us about history, her voice changed. She loved history. She loved to read about it, think about it, talk about it, and share it with others. She never just lectured; she talked with her hands and kept our attention with her facial expressions. She led us on a grand tour. (Audrey)

When studying for my teaching credential, I had an amazing, charismatic education professor. I remember his flashing smile, resonant voice, exuberant spirit, bright eye contact, and resonant voice, and I envision his imposing presence: tall, shoulders back, relaxed, and confident. He owned the subject and the classroom; he worked the room easily, comfortably. He focused on us, his students, and not on himself. It was marvelous to sit in his classroom and learn how to teach from watching him.

Fast-forward thirty years and 2,000 miles away, and in a curious twist of fate, my education professor's granddaughter sat in my teacher education classes ready to learn how to teach—from me, a humbling responsibility to be sure. I used to chide her that if she didn't like the methods I taught, she could blame her grandfather because I learned much of what I knew about teaching from him. When the time came to observe her student teach, it was déjà vu— like sitting once again in her grandfather's class.

She had the same warm smile, sense of presence, relaxed eye contact, meaningful gestures, and passion for her subject and the students. She worked magic with her students in rapt attention, clearly comfortable in her role, even as a novice teacher. Turning to my observation notes, I summed it up this way: "Teaching is in your genes!" She is one of the lucky ones. In truth, there was not much I needed to teach her; she possessed natural teaching skill from the start.

All teachers may not be born with a natural presence or engaging enthusiasm that grabs and holds student attention, but they can develop many such skills variously suited to their own personality. I've seen it repeatedly. Teachers can develop their natural characteristics to convey enthusiasm and confidence, much like an actor portrays a role on stage (Tauber and Mester 2006).

Although acting a role, like wearing a curly red clown wig or jumping on a desk, is sure to gain students' attention, some conscientious teachers might recoil at this idea, protesting that they are in the classroom to teach, not entertain. They make a good point. Education is serious work, but the notion of teacher acting deserves a second look. After all, how many people would sit through a play if the performers stood on the stage and merely recited their lines with no expression, gestures, passion, or willingness to engage the audience?

■ He brought the world of mathematics alive day in and day out. He connected with us and taught with expression and passion. By example he showed that anything can be conquered. During my seventh-grade year, he had a brain tumor removed successfully. He sustained severe nerve damage in the operation. A right-hander, he learned to become a southpaw. His speech was severely impaired, but he never once showed me that he couldn't still teach with expression and passion. In fact, I think his determination, experiences, and humility made him an even better teacher! (Alex)

The word *acting* might better be termed *animated* when referring to mannerisms and facial expressions that draw students to the teacher and, more important, into the content. For example, demonstrative arm and hand gestures can serve to clearly emphasize critical points. Well-placed facial expressions, like broad smiles or raised eyebrows, and changing vocal pitch from excited oratory to hushed whisper can convey the intrigue of an idea. These animated responses communicate energy and passion, lending credibility to the teacher and authenticity to the content. Students describe it as "coming alive" in class.

■ The teacher seemed to feel the subject. He came alive on the stage. The subject was history of the 1960s, and he grew up during that time. Once he even showed slides of himself in that style of dress. It was very amusing. He talked from firsthand knowledge through lectures that spoke of not only events and dates but also character, honor, and pride. (Ben)

VOCAL QUALITY

In the quest to bring subject matter alive, teachers talk a lot; some would say they talk too much. When they want to emphasize a point, however, spirited teachers, like good performers, harness the power of vocal pitch, intentionally fine-tuning its strength and intensity.

I learned a lesson from my own vocal blunders about the importance of varying my vocal pitch during a lecture. I tend to talk loudly in the classroom (my family calls it my teacher's voice), reasoning that all students from the front to the back row need to hear my carefully crafted comments. I discovered the true extent of my vocal projection one semester when I taught a class on the highest floor of a tower adjacent to the library. Arriving early one day, I threw open the tower window, and, like a cloistered Rapunzel, I surveyed the campus far below and savored the late afternoon breeze.

When class got under way, I introduced the day's lesson with my usual robust volume. A few minutes later, a couple of students walked in late, razzing me that they hadn't missed anything because they could hear my introduction from outside the tower, four stories below. Other students nodded in agreement, and we all had a good laugh at my expense. I decided that teachers can better emphasize important points when they vary volume and tone.

■ When he read aloud in class, his voice would convey his deep feeling and attachment to the work itself. For the sermon "Sinners in the Hands of an Angry God," he gave it like a real sermon. For "The Scarlet Letter," he walked in one day and calmly stated that Hester caused the whole thing—which led to a huge class debate in seconds. He knew that all students didn't love English, so he made it come alive. (Laura)

KNOWLEDGE AND DEPTH

Deep and broad teacher content knowledge is somewhat akin to actors who know their character and lines cold. Actors and teachers cannot effectively share what they don't know well or experience deeply. Effective teachers never stop learning or weaving new insights through the classroom fabric. Simply put, proficient teachers can't hold back, and they inspire students to love the subject as well.

■ First and foremost, there can be no teacher with a greater knowledge of the subject than Professor B. He was by far the most fascinating lecturer I have witnessed, and his depth, energy, and spirit spewed out every day. His classes were always full—always. (Steven)

Teachers broaden and deepen their knowledge through reading, attending selected conferences, interacting with other teachers, experiencing life, researching beyond the text, and traveling. I appreciated the vital role of life experience and travel for enhancing teacher depth when my husband and some friends scheduled a trip to China. I wanted to go, of course, but I wrestled with some guilt. After all, I would leave behind volumes of work, lessons to prepare, writing to do, and new texts to digest for the upcoming school year. The trip would simply be a vacation, for I naively reasoned that traveling to China would have no connection with my work—after all, I did not teach world history.

A few weeks before the scheduled trip, the college president stopped me on campus and said something that stuck with me. He had heard about my upcoming trip and wished me safe travel. Then he looked at me and purposefully added, "Travel always makes a person a better teacher." He was right, of course, for each year I have used insights and examples gleaned from that and other trips to better inform my teaching and interaction with diverse students.

■ During that class, I realized the importance of visual imaging. The Middle East is such an incredibly diverse area, and geography ended up being much more than countries and capitals! He made all of our studies "live." He relied extensively on videotape that he had shot while spending many years in the Middle East, and he gave the class packets of interesting materials every day. Never did he just "lecture" to us. (Aaron)

TEACHING STYLES AND KIDS

A colleague shared her surprising interview with a new applicant to teacher education. After the customary discussion of requirements, the young applicant asked an ironic but telling question: "Do you have to like kids to be a teacher?" How do you answer such a basic yet phenomenal question and remove the practice of teaching from the passion for kids? You can't. Whatever a teacher's unique style, kids are the only reason to become a teacher and the only reason to continue.

■ He got into his teaching. He took us to the fields to explain science and nature. He wanted us to see for ourselves what we were learning, not just read about it. He loved being in the classroom with "his" kids. He loved seeing our minds develop. He loved watching us grow, and he loved being a part of it all. He loved to teach; it was evident to all of us, even as seventh graders. (Jacob)

Teachers who love kids become energized and renewed in their presence, and a teacher's natural style revives. I once had an illuminating conversation with a friend and surgeon. He related his experience with the fatigue demon that shadows him into the operating room. He admitted that when scheduled to operate, he can be exhausted and reluctant to scrub in. Yet no matter how tired he feels, once he enters the operating room, considers the patient, and begins his work, something magical and mystical takes over, and his passion for helping the patient consumes his fatigue. It is simply gone. He feels alert, energized, and in charge of the operating room.

I identified with him, for I've recognized the same feelings, now and then, before an upcoming class. The feeling is a dense fog of fatigue that requires me to shake it off and be at the top of my teaching game. But when I walk through the classroom door, greet my students, and begin to interact with them, the fatigue dissolves effortlessly, and I feel the creative juices return.

How can it be explained? A teacher's passion for challenging minds and sharing ideas resides deep inside and bubbles up primarily in the company of students. Deep passion can't help but show and inspire. Loving the students, loving the subject, and loving the interaction—it's a teacher's style, and it shows.

KEY IDEAS
✓ Vastly different teaching styles can be equally effective if sincere, authentic, appropriate, and student centered.
✓ "Stage presence" is a useful art to be cultivated and integrated within a teacher's unique style.
✓ Teachers develop passion for their subject areas through extensive study, travel, and meaningful life experience. Passion shows and engages student enthusiasm.
✓ Warm, enthusiastic greetings reel in students from the tentacles of distractions to the deck of the classroom.

Teacher and Student Gender

■ For some unknown reason, I had a lot of trouble in third grade. I seemed to have a problem with everything we were learning. My cursive letters wouldn't slant, I couldn't multiply or divide, and all of my poems and stories would never come out sounding the way that I wanted them to. Thinking about this, I have memories of my teacher. I can see her hand, her wedding band shining and her short fingernails resting on my desk as she leans over to help me with yet another problem, and the smell of her perfume is still so fresh, just as if she was leaning over me now to help me with handwriting. (Sarah)

STUDENTS NOTICE

The smell of perfume speaks to the unique gender characteristics linked to female and male teachers that lace classroom life with an endearing assortment of "she and he" personality traits, temperaments, clothing styles, hairdos, viewpoints, and mannerisms. Make no mistake, students notice them all, for both genders.

■ She was a very classy person—always presenting herself well (nice clothes, well groomed, etc.). (Natalie)

■ He was an older, fifty- to fifty-five-year-old, bearded, redheaded, bespectacled man. He was quite inspirational to say the least. (Michelle)

I recognized that students notice their teachers' appearance at a point in my high school teaching career when my hairdresser suggested that I adopt a new hairstyle. "Your hair is too perfect," she remarked as she purposefully tousled my locks, "and the styles are more natural now—a little more messy." Gazing at my new image in the mirror, I was a bit startled that my neatly coifed hair was now sticking up and out as if I had just emerged from a wind tunnel. Smiling, my hairdresser convinced me that my new look mimicked current trends.

The next morning as I readied for school, I dried my hair, and instead of crafting each strand into perfect symmetry, I flipped my head upside down, shook it back and forth, ran my lightly waxed fingers through my hair, and completed the grooming session with a bit of hairspray before dashing out the door. I half expected my high school students to laugh at me; but instead, spilling into the classroom, they quickly commented on my new look: "Hey Mrs. Balli, I like your hair today." And thus, variations on my messy hairdo remained for many years. Without a doubt, students notice everything about their teachers.

■ I remember her warmth and sincerity and also her beauty. She was one of the most beautiful women I had ever seen or at least that was what I thought at the time. (Lauren)

DOES TEACHER GENDER MATTER?

With the understanding that students notice everything about a teacher's appearance, personality, and mannerisms, does it otherwise matter to students if their teacher is a male or a female? Of the 148 essays excerpted throughout this book, eighty-five portrayed female teachers and sixty-two described male teachers. Male teachers represented 42 percent of the essays even though, at this writing, males make up 25 percent of the K–12 teacher workforce and 9 percent of the elementary schoolteacher workforce (U.S. Department of Education 2008).

Does that mean that male teachers are better liked, more remembered, or deemed excellent more often than are female teachers? Probably not. More likely, it is possible that male teachers stand out in some student memories because of their novelty, particularly in elementary classrooms.

Our daughter and son had a male teacher for first grade. Like the grade he taught, Mr. Evans was unconventional in every way. Take his clothes, for example. His wife, who worked in the school office, sewed a full line of brightly colored ties for Mr. Evans with matching outfits for herself. The first graders were treated to a daily round of eye-catching rainbow colors and extravagant prints to spark their visual imaginations.

With a vibrant personality to complement his ties, Mr. Evans approached teaching with enthusiastic drive, organizing his curriculum with exceptional rigor by first-grade standards. His first-rate teaching skills earned him several awards throughout his long and distinguished career.

Our children differed somewhat in their response to Mr. Evans's nononsense approach. Kevin missed the first day of school because of illness, and Mr. Evans, not wanting Kevin to lose a moment of phonics instruction, actually visited us at home on that first afternoon to teach pajama-clad Kevin his initial lesson in sounds and letters with a slew of songs and motions. Mr. Evans called Kevin "hotshot" from day one and pressed him to read more and memorize more, which served him well years later.

On the other hand, excellent female teachers have a deep impact on their students as well, and our daughter Karen preferred the laid-back, warm, and nurturing tone set by her second-grade teacher, Mrs. Anderson. Mrs. Anderson (illuminated in an earlier chapter) filled a "home away from home" role for Karen. So, all told, do male students, particularly young male students, prefer male teacher role models and likewise with female students and teachers? Not necessarily.

Our granddaughter Megan, now in fifth grade, reminisced fondly about Mr. Davis, her only male teacher thus far. Mr. Davis, an adroit basketball player, taught second grade and empowered his students to do their best by repeatedly invoking a basketball metaphor. His mantra was, "Practice, and the ball bounces high. Neglect practice, and the ball bounces low and rolls away." Throughout the school year, if student motivation waned, Mr. Davis galvanized perseverance with his signature saying, "Bounce the ball higher!" Megan, a tall, budding athlete, readily identified with this strategy and with Mr. Davis.

How much does it matter to students whether they have a male or a female teacher? Does gender influence teaching and learning in subtle ways? Clearly, teachers and students connect for a host of reasons that defy gender categories, gender matching, and gender theories. Nevertheless, gender-related characteristics, role modeling, and gender stereotyping are worth mining for ways in which they variously influence classroom life.

TEACHER GENDER AND AFFECTIVE QUALITIES

The students whose teacher vignettes are included in this book remembered both male and female teachers for exceptional teaching skills. Among a range of affective qualities, students depicted both male and female teachers as a friend. Both male and female students occasionally used precise descriptors like *warm, soothing, openhearted, thoughtful,* and *compassionate* to set female teachers apart, while the broader affective term *caring* characterized both teacher genders.

Females

- She had an open ear and an open heart with the warmest voice, soothing and comforting. She was kind and compassionate. It felt like she was your personal cheering section, rooting for you through every tough or easy situation. I am grateful to her, and I hope I can be as caring and thoughtful as she is. (Samantha)

Males

- He was wise—directed, focused—and most of all he really cared, evident by his actions in the classroom and his personality. Overall, he cared about me at a time in my life when I felt like the world was against me—when I thought I was all alone. (Sam)

FAMILY ROLE MODELS

Among the teacher gender characteristics noticed by students, some are specifically tied to valued family members. Teachers may unknowingly make a natural connection with a student who has a family member similar in appearance and personality, and students identify with such a teacher, male or female, who fills the familiar space of someone important in the student's life—a mother, father, or grandparent, as in the following examples.

■ I'm not sure what made him so special, but I always looked forward to going to his class. I think I liked him because he was such a nice old guy. He reminded me of my grandpa. He coached the women's cross-country team, and even though he was too old to run, he followed them in his car as they ran down the street. He was a good teacher, not spectacular, but he inspired me go into the teaching profession. (Jordan)

■ My first-grade teacher reminded me of my grandmother. The year was a big adjustment for me because I wasn't used to being away from my mother for all day, and I often came to school crying. My teacher helped me feel better by letting me sit on her lap, putting a smiley-faced button on my shirt, and telling me of all the fun activities we would be doing that day. After a few weeks, I stopped crying every day because I looked forward to school. (Jessica)

PROFESSIONAL ROLE MODELS

Male and female teachers can—and often do—function as gender-specific professional role models. In their essays, male students wrote about male teachers more than twice as often as they wrote about female teachers. Likewise, female students wrote twice as often about female teachers. When students identify with a professional role model of like gender, it sharpens their observations with a vision of who they can become.

Teachers may be unaware that their daily persona and actions are powerful examples for those students who have adopted the teacher as a professional role model. I recall a surprising conversation with the mother of one of my former high school students who was just entering the job market. The mother shared her daughter's expressed commitment to be a "professional like Mrs. Balli." Taken aback, I remembered this young woman as one of my more challenging students, regularly a classroom distraction, one who left me at wit's end more often than not. As teachers, we rarely understand the extent of our professional influence, and it often intersects along gender lines.

Female Professional

■ I feel lucky to have had her as my French teacher. She had a huge impact on my life, and I can only imagine the impact she had on the lives of other students. From her ingenuity, I was inspired to look for unique ways to develop interest in learning like she did for me. I will do my best to model myself as a teacher from what I learned from her. (Veronica)

Male Professional

■ His personality conveys everything I would like to be as a teacher. In every aspect, he inspired me to push myself harder, and the hard work and persistence that he instilled is what I want to pass on to other students someday. He will always be instrumental in my quest to learn the best way to teach young minds, and his was the single most motivational class for me to be an outstanding educator. (Anthony)

GENDER STEREOTYPES

Despite a tendency for females and males to admire exemplary people within their own gender, society and the media have perpetuated gender role stereotyping over time, and those attitudes eventually filter down to students. Teachers can help break down barriers and reverse unrestrained gender stereotypes through example and attitudes that honor both genders. The following vignette offers insight on a teacher's purposeful attempt to cut through gender stereotypes.

■ My teacher and his wife lived in a very poor part of town. He said that there were guns going off and a lot of their windows had been shot out, and I said, "Aren't you afraid your wife might get hurt?" He said "Heck, no, she's tough enough to take care of herself; it's me that she needs to worry about." The reason I love this story is because in the last few years I have become more and more of a feminist, and he was very aware of the limitations society puts on women, and he always made it a point to break those down. (Sophia)

Gender stereotyping can interfere with students' aspirations to enter professions that are normally viewed as gender specific. Among the stereotypes perpetuated about gender-specific jobs, the teaching profession is rampant with gender patterns. Women, for example, remain underrepresented in college teaching, while men remain underrepresented in elementary teaching. Stereotyping can discourage all but the most tenacious from pursuing their ambitions. In interviews with seventeen male elementary teachers, Cushman (2005) found that twelve of them did not begin their career in elementary classrooms, citing the cautionary reactions of friends and relatives to their professional goals.

Despite the fact that both our son and daughter had a male first-grade teacher and that I believe men who teach young children can make a positive difference in children's lives, I got tangled in my own stereotype web when two of my students shared their plans to teach in the primary grades. The first, a female student, stopped by my office to announce her decision to teach first grade. I gushed about her skills, her warmth, and her gentle nature, all well suited to young students. Later, a male student stopped by to share his aspirations to teach first grade. I smiled affirmatively, adding, "Oh, really," a code phrase for polite surprise. My conditioned response had no basis in reality or his suitability for elementary teaching.

According to the National Education Association, the number of men teaching in U.S. schools is falling to a forty-year low. As stated earlier, 25 percent of the nation's 3 million teachers are men, and for elementary teachers, only 9 percent are men, down from 18 percent in 1981 (National Education Association 2008). To counter teacher gender stereotypes, male elementary education majors at the University of Missouri, along with first-year male teachers, started an organization aimed to increase the number of male elementary teachers and to raise public awareness about excellence found among practicing male elementary teachers.

The student organization sponsors research on the differences between male and female brain functioning. They implement gender-specific instructional strategies during student teaching and their first year of practice that are specifically designed to foster increased learning. The members suggest that both male and female elementary students need positive male role models during their formative years. According to the men in the group, if students see only female teachers in elementary school, students may perceive that school and learning are not as important for boys as for girls (University of Missouri–Columbia 2007).

GENDER BIAS

■ If she was partial to a particular gender, she never showed it. She was caring and showed a great deal of interest in each individual student. (Liz)

Turning from teacher gender to student gender, many teachers are surprised to discover subtle differences in the way they respond to male and female students. While teachers intend to respond equally to all students, videotaping carried out in classrooms revealed that teachers tend to give boys more attention, calling on them more often and giving them more feedback (Sadker and Sadker 1994). When teachers became aware of this situation, they indicated that boys solicit more attention from teachers because boys raise their hands more often and generally engage in more disruptive behavior.

Effective teachers remedy gender inequities by deliberately implementing procedures to alternately call on male and female students. They further strengthen equality by organizing learning materials that portray men and women in ways that counter stereotypes and encourage female students to consider advanced courses in math and science in greater numbers.

Educators are making good progress in this endeavor. University of Wisconsin researchers compared the performance of 7 million students from grades 2 through 11 and found that girls scored as well in mathematics on standardized tests as did boys at every grade level (Hyde et al. 2008). Female mathematics scores rose significantly, and, fortunately, male mathematics scores did not drop.

I have seen growth in the number of female math and science teacher education students in the past decade due, in part, to more careful attention in dispelling gender bias. Female math or science teachers often have their choice of teaching positions anywhere there is an opening. It speaks well of school districts that encourage gender equity, with female teachers becoming more visible in these subjects areas to serve as role models for female students.

STUDENT GENDER AND LEARNING

Whatever their gender, teachers would do well to seriously consider how student gender relates to learning. Is it possible for equality to be carried to extreme? Do male and female students differ at all in their interests and pathways for learning? If so, can teachers discern and use gender-based interests and learning styles to optimize student learning in all subject areas? Should teachers recognize and acknowledge certain gender differences or press boys and girls into identical learning strategy molds?

I've observed gender-related interests play out quite naturally in our family. For example, our four granddaughters showcase a mountain of stuffed animals in their bedrooms. Our grandson displays pirate ships and Transformers. Our granddaughters like to draw and write stories. Our grandson climbs on people and furniture. Recently, our grandson insisted that I ride with him on the Tower of Terror at Disneyland while his sister pointed out the nearest exit in case I got too nervous. Lest I reduce gender interests to simplistic biased characterizations, I'm reminded that our oldest granddaughter, Megan, handled pythons and rats at summer camp, and our grandson, Jack, has a few stuffed animals of his own, some with girl names.

When it comes to schooling, do gender, interests, and learning style relate to each other in some way? Do parents and grandparents teach girls and boys to appreciate stereotypical pastimes and toys, or are girls and boys hardwired differently? If so, how can teachers use gender research to strengthen classroom community and learning?

According to King and Gurian (2006), brain research illuminates specific cortical differences associated with gender, with girls' brains emphasizing verbal-emotive processing, making girls better able to sit still, listen, and take notes, while boys' brains accentuate spatial-mechanical functioning, making them more attuned to physical activities. Furthermore, while girls' brains cross talk between hemispheres, making them better able to multitask, boys' brains compartmentalize information, making them naturally focus more efficiently on one thing at a time.

Applied in the classroom, more girls will be content to quietly organize words and punctuation in a notebook, and more boys will thrive on spacing word cards in the correct order on the classroom floor. Both genders learn the words, meeting the objective through different pathways. While girls may enjoy literature circles with other girls to discuss a fantasy book on unicorns, boys might prefer literature circles with other boys to discuss a book about car racing. Both genders will read but engage in different topics. While girls may write a story about friends, boys might enjoy writing about an action-packed adventure. While there are decided exceptions, girls communicate with more words, and boys communicate with more action (King and Gurian 2006).

■ This teacher shunned traditional textbooks and instead taught through literature. One book we read was *The Hobbit.* Then we did group projects of anything we wanted to that related to the book. Our girl's group retold the story as a picture book, and we drew illustrations. One of the boy's groups built a life-sized papier-mâché character taken from the story. (Vicky)

Perceptive teachers with success expectations for all students understand and celebrate these differences, weaving them purposefully into classroom routines instead of railing against them in attempts to equalize all activities in education. Teachers who understand male and female brain functioning can differentiate activities to take advantage of natural tendencies, and when teachers have done so, the boys, who usually lag behind girls in all areas of literacy, show remarkable gains in achievement (King and Gurian 2006).

TEACHER GENDER AND STUDENT LEARNING

If we embrace documented differences in the way males and females learn, would it follow that matching student gender with teacher gender could influence learning in some way? In the reality of classroom life, situations arise in which gender matching is appropriate and invaluable, particularly when it comes to responding to students' personal problems, problems that wreck havoc with learning.

■ She began support groups for students who needed help with personal problems. She set up groups for pregnancy, weight loss, and kids of divorced parents. Many former students came back to tell her how much they learned and how they have succeeded because of her. She motivated students who had never previously succeeded in school before. (Carol)

Aside from personal issues, Dee's (2006) analysis of the National Education Longitudinal Survey found that teacher gender does influence academics to a small degree at least for middle school students. With data from more than 20,000 eighth graders and their teachers, Dee found that boys who had male teachers and girls who had female teachers did slightly better in science, English, and social studies than did those students who were not gender matched with their teachers. This finding held after accounting for class size, ethnicity, teacher certification, and teacher experience.

Despite small achievement gains, the shortage of male teachers makes gender matching not only impractical but realistically undesirable as well. Both male and female students benefit from interaction with male and female teachers as students mature into adults. But while systematic student and teacher gender matching is unrealistic, a growing number of public schools do offer a selection of single-sex classes to harness the developmental needs and interests of male and female students (National Association for Single Sex Public Education 2008).

In fact, early in my career, I enjoyed a most adventurous and carefree teaching experience—a single-sex male home economics high school course. In 1980, home economics traditionally comprised females, mainly if not exclusively. As an experiment, I organized a males-only course, reasoning that with the growing number of women in the workforce, men needed the skills to manage the home-front tasks primarily carried out by women. Most important, they needed to learn these skills without being intimidated or distracted by females in the same class.

I assembled a group of eight to ten young men brave enough to enroll in a "girl class" as it was prominently labeled at the time. Together we forged an untapped journey intended to develop their skills in managing household tasks on their own. We explored basic nutrition and meal preparation, and the guys became adept at preparing chili, lasagna, soup, and other "super bowl" soul food. They learned to sew, using their natural mechanical ability to effectively master a sewing machine. One student made a long slip for his girlfriend who couldn't locate just the right one to match the formal dress she chose for a school party. The guys finished the course learning how to iron, to budget, and to raise children.

Years later, I reaped the results of this experiment when I encountered one of my former males-only home economics students. He introduced me to his wife and two adorable children. With compelling pride, he declared that his children's good manners stemmed in part from what he had learned about child development years ago in our class. "Who says parenting comes naturally?" His wife acknowledged his fatherly forte.

Several years later, I encountered another one of my males-only students at a conference. A longtime teacher and then principal, he strode confidently into the meeting room dressed neatly in a white shirt and tie. Greeting me warmly and introducing me to his friends, he called everyone's attention to his perfectly pressed shirt that had emerged disheveled from his suitcase the night before. He entertained us with hilarious descriptions of his expertise in ironing wrinkled shirts, assuring us that he is always dressed for success in his administrative role.

EXCELLENCE ACROSS GENDER

Teachers and students end up together in classrooms without much choice in gender mix. The chance assortment of male and female teachers and students add an enjoyable melting pot of personality, style, and interest to classroom life. It's a good thing. Male and female teacher representation at all grade levels can only broaden and strengthen a student's educational experience.

All told, students connect with teachers, whether male or female, for mysterious reasons that defy description. For teachers, the key is not whether they are male or female but rather the extent to which they are authentic and determined to do their best work every day, offering their unique gifts, and embracing the diverse hand of students they are dealt at the beginning of the school year. A winning year lies not so much in what is dealt as in playing the game with authenticity, purpose, and passion.

> A teacher's purpose is not to create students in his [or her] own image, but to develop students who can create their own image.
>
> —Author unknown

KEY IDEAS

✓ Appreciating and celebrating gender diversity at all grade levels enhances the flavor of classroom life for both teachers and students.

✓ Recognizing male and female students equally, despite bids for attention, ensures unbiased relationships and fair opportunities for both genders.

✓ Understanding gender differences in interests and learning styles helps teachers appropriately differentiate activities and groupings to take advantage of the best in both genders.

✓ Providing male and female role models in all fields encourages male and female students to explore diverse endeavors.

12

Not Like Some Teachers

■ Even though I was a sincere student, I was terrified of any kind of
math or science. This teacher crossed the line from teaching math
and science to teaching students. Unlike some teachers who are willing to let their students fall by the wayside, this teacher took an interest in each of us. I can't recall a single time when he was too busy
to help me, and he treated me with kindness whether I succeeded or
failed in his classes. By the time I graduated, I no longer had an overwhelming fear of math. By helping me overcome an anxiety, he
taught me a life lesson—simple but worthy: never be afraid to try;
you might surprise yourself by succeeding. (Heather)

ROLE EXPECTATIONS

Students have a way of depicting contrasting sentiments about excellent and
mediocre teachers with acute clarity and choice descriptions. Heather, for example, used the phrase "let their students fall by the wayside" to conjure up
images of cold, heartless teachers whose students languish in the classroom
ditch. Ouch. On the other hand, some dramatic teacher descriptions have
more benign meanings. Case in point: our granddaughter Megan candidly re-
ferred to the "scary" teacher at school, and I asked, "What do you mean by
scary?" "Well, she comes up behind you when you're doing your work and
says, 'Boo.'"

151

Truth be told, teachers vary in disposition and practice, and at times we can be attentive or indifferent, wise or mindless, prepared or unready. Whether we like it or not, students scrutinize and know us well, and in *Saturday Night Live* fashion, students can comically imitate teacher foibles and mannerisms with astounding accuracy. Because student perceptions mirror their reality and because they hold contrasting images of excellent and mediocre teachers, it is useful to explore the tenor of how teachers come across to students and how teachers meet or do not meet student expectations.

In a broad sense, we all hold expectations for our world and the people we meet based on years of observation and experience. For example, we have an idea of what to expect from encounters with certain people—doctors, gangsters, lawyers, or teachers—based on stories we have heard or interactions we have had. We hold these expectations based on our understanding of a particular role and the typical behavior for the role (Biddle 1979). Once informed or experienced, we envision what to expect in upcoming encounters. When a particular encounter decidedly exceeds our role expectations, we are caught off guard, pleasantly surprised, like receiving an unexpected and satisfying gift.

Collectively, we hold several common expectations for the role of a teacher, the conveyor of wisdom who occupies a large space in the fabric of society. We expect that teachers will practice conventional instructional methods that inform and guide the multitude of students who pass through classrooms year after year. We expect that teachers like to work with children, adolescents, or young adults.

Students, as the people most closely associated with teachers, fashion their own set of nuanced beliefs based on year after year of interactions with teachers. So then, when teachers exceed student expectations, when students enter classrooms and win the "teacher lottery," it creates an intriguing sense of dissonance when they compare those exceptional teachers with the more ordinary or mediocre teachers they have encountered.

JUXTAPOSITIONS

Across every school district, society expects teachers to provide information, grant report cards, organize learning materials, and administer discipline when necessary. But for students, teaching is more than working out the mechanical elements of a job description; and those teachers who are a cut above the rest, those who are extraordinary rather than ordinary, occupy a prime place in students' memories. And thus some of the students whose memories make up this book juxtaposed contrasting teacher descriptions in a way that sliced mediocre teachers from extraordinary ones, much like slicing a bad spot from an apple.

For example, in the opening vignette for this chapter, Heather juxtaposed her "never too busy" teacher with teachers who "are willing to let their students fall by the wayside." In another example, from the opening vignette in chapter 1, Becky described a funny-looking boy who wore coke-bottle glasses. In Becky's portrayal of her teacher's attitude, she juxtaposed her expectations for typical teachers who could let teasing slide by with a description of her exemplary teacher who would not.

■ I believe he was given a chance to really develop despite his looks. Most kids would have been making fun of him, and the typical teacher would just let this kind of treatment slide. Our teacher would not and did not let this happen. (Becky)

Juxtaposition places words, ideas, or images next to one another especially for purposes of comparison or contrast (Clark 2005). The result creates an unsettling dissonance, forcing a pause, like a long comma, to contemplate the incongruities created by the contrast (Festinger 1957). Consider the following stark examples: a photograph of the American flag juxtaposed amidst the World Trade Center debris, a description of African slaves as bound and bleeding at the foot of civilized and Christianized humanity in the literary classic *Uncle Tom's Cabin* (Stowe 1852), and a film's instrumental rendition of "Nearer My God to Thee" while the frigid ocean swallowed the *Titanic* (Cameron and Landau 1997).

Juxtapositions intrigue the mind, throwing it slightly or decidedly off balance into a state of dissonance that seeks resolution. The purpose of juxtaposition is accomplished when we reflect on the juxtaposed words, descriptions, or images, and in the reflecting, we form deeper insights about an issue. For example, in contemplating teachers who let their students fall by the wayside, we can reflect on an academic wilderness and wonder what it means for students to fall by the wayside; how and why a teacher lets that happen; how students, abandoned on the wayside, get back on track; or how teachers might sew protective nets to catch students at the precipice of a classroom wayside experience.

What follows are juxtaposed descriptions of teachers set in the context of a variety of classroom situations. The juxtapositions invite us to pause and reflect on the contrasts between good and not-so-good teachers from the perspective of student experience and expectations. The descriptions illuminate the dichotomies of teaching and teachers—the mediocre teachers who fall short juxtaposed with the extraordinary teachers who exceed.

ON A PEDESTAL

■ Speaking for myself and probably the rest of his students, you could talk with him about anything. He wasn't up on the pedestal that many teachers seem to be on. He talked about things that we wanted to talk about. I believe that he wasn't there just for a paycheck because he had such a great time teaching. (James)

If students, in their admiration, elevate a teacher to a respected position on a metaphorical pedestal, we acknowledge that the teacher must be extraordinary in some way. The teacher must be head and shoulders above other teachers, especially when the teacher description is juxtaposed with a description of a power-hungry teacher, one who ascends a self-made pedestal, intent on controlling unsuspecting students.

Our son-in-law, Scott, encountered a power-hungry, pedestal-climbing teacher in one of his college classes during the time when he diligently pursued a business degree before his upcoming marriage to our daughter, Karen. His studies, however, were the least of Scott's challenges. More burdensome, Scott had to withstand Dr. K, his major professor and adviser, reputed to preside like a cavalier dictator over students at his royal mercy. Scott's congenial nature navigated this kingdom state with grace, as he minded his own studies, knuckling down and avoiding conflict.

During one class period, however, Dr. K dashed off a long series of crucial business concepts, rapidly scrawling them across the board, as illegibly as a physician's prescription. Unable to keep pace, Scott approached Dr. K with characteristic courtesy to seek clarification after class. Unlike most teachers who delight in a student's overtures of interest, Dr. K dismissed Scott's inquiry, indicating that Scott had missed the sufficient information posted on the board.

Dr. K further ruled that he would not offer Scott additional assistance until he submitted an ophthalmologist's letter indicating whether he needed glasses—appalling but true. Dr. K's approach was as subtle as a garlic sand-wich. Although Scott continued to take required classes from this calloused professor, his "I know everything attitude" prompted Scott to choose another adviser to guide his academic journey to its successful conclusion.

KNOW-IT-ALL

■ She was not one to talk down to people. She shared her knowledge in a nonarrogant, nonboastful way, not in an "I know everything atti-tude" like some teachers. (Kara)

Teachers pride themselves on having a firm grasp of their subject areas, and like most teachers, I feel unsettled when I don't know everything about a course assigned to my teaching schedule. I want to be competent when interacting with students who have a right to gain new insights from me. When uncertain, it's tempting to fake it, to act like I know everything when I really don't. I learned through humbling experience that I don't know everything and that my students know more than I do about some things, and that it is okay.

For example, I taught a computer class to aspiring teachers at a time when the Internet emerged in its earliest infancy. I required a textbook, about the size of a small phone book, that included every single World Wide Web ad-dress in play at that early time. I taught my college students the basic steps for how to send and receive e-mail, a worthy lesson plan in the early 1990s—a ridiculous lesson by today's standards.

Within a few years, my most savvy students, young and eager experimenters, knew much more about computer technology than I did. Initially, I panicked, but rather than berating myself and continuing with an "I know everything" charade, I enlisted my students in a learning community where we explored rapid advances in technology together and taught each other. When I admitted to myself and others that I did not know everything, I finally relaxed and en-joyed facilitating a productive class. I have come to appreciate learning from my students while preserving my confidence and enhancing theirs.

ADMITTING MISTAKES

In their role as the leaders of classroom life, it may at times be difficult for teachers to acknowledge that they were wrong about a decision, a strategy, or an interaction. Students have come to expect that teachers characteristically maintain their demeanor as not only in charge but also correct in what they do and say. When teachers authentically and unexpectedly apologize, students take notice.

■ One time, he generalized the effect of social groups on eating disorders and used sororities as the target for his generalization. I disagreed with his statement and wrote him a polite letter about it, and he apologized for what he said in front of the class. I was shocked that a teacher would ever admit he was wrong in front of the class. (Nancy)

Students welcome teacher apologies, and honest admissions of error strengthen authenticity. I recall one disastrous summer when I taught an intensive two-week course to a group of high school teachers. The course covered an entire semester's worth of content. As sometimes happens in an intensive course, we regularly got sidetracked from the prescribed curriculum to a variety of tangential, lively discussions and debates. It is immensely stimulating to teach practicing teachers because their variety of real-world, immediate classroom experience enriches and fills every class period from opening comments to closing remarks.

And so, as the course rapidly neared the last half hour of the final day, I had not yet explained a major project requirement that was to be completed that fall in their classrooms and submitted to me electronically. As I distributed handouts and begin to explain the postcourse project, I quickly recognized my error in waiting so long to unfold this final task. Naturally, students were anxious to get home, many having come from great distance to stay nearby the university for the full two weeks.

Conscientious to a fault, they peppered me with detailed questions about misunderstandings that tested my resolve not to throw the whole project in the trash. Working through the complex procedures, I felt a palpable sense of tension among the group. I did what I could to make the best of a bad situation and ultimately apologized to the class for my poor planning in introducing this component of the course so late in the game. Once I apologized, the frozen tension began to melt away as the warmth returned and we worked through a modified and reasonable assignment that matched the time for explanation and understanding.

SPEWING FACTS

■ We had very few busywork assignments. We constantly did projects and cooperative activities. A lot of the lessons were not just the teacher standing up and spewing facts but rather an interactive conversation. Everything we did as a class had a purpose. Those purposes were always made clear to us. (Margaret)

Picture a classroom run by a teacher who spews facts that hold zero appeal. My father languished in many such classrooms. During the 1930s Depression leading up to World War II, most teachers had little time or patience for instruction beyond the busywork of basic facts—readin', writin', and 'rithmetic, as traditional schooling came to be known. Juxtaposed with this, my father fondly remembers Len Smith, his English teacher extraordinaire during the Depression years.

Mr. Smith taught a cut above other teachers; he taught with humor and variety during a dark and dismal time in our nation's history. Unlike my father's other more serious "spewing facts" teachers, Mr. Smith wrapped his class with essential concepts as well as lighthearted fun, switching effortlessly between Martin Luther King passion and Jay Leno risqué in a matter of minutes.

Early one fall, shortly before Franklin Roosevelt's controversial third run for the presidency, Mr. Smith randomly divided his students into an equal number of Democrats and Republicans without regard to their parents' actual affiliation. He assigned the students to write an essay detailing what their respective candidates could provide to benefit all American citizens. My father recalls that his essay effused with tongue-in-cheek stuff, including "all the women in America would be pleased as patriots to have Eleanor running the country again instead of a man" and "pet owners would love to have Fala back in the White House for a third term of dog stories."

Dad remembers Mr. Smith doubled over with laughter, setting the tone as the rest of the class boisterously joined the fray. The assignment and the class possessed serious elements, to be sure, but unlike many other teachers of his era, Mr. Smith did not just spew serious facts to mirror the times; rather, he celebrated his students' creativity. When a teacher is out of the ordinary, students learn life lessons more comprehensive than those offered by colorless facts, lessons like it's possible to have fun even during a national depression, as my father relived, nearly seventy years later.

■ She addressed controversial topics in her class to spark discussion
and debate. She demanded that we think about tough moral issues
with long-term projects. Unlike some teachers, she made us interested in the subject rather than just regurgitating colorless theories
and facts. (Faith)

Effective classrooms are more than repositories for colorless facts. Students
dream of classrooms where schooling is not a continuous round of business
as usual but is laced as well with elements of surprise. This notion bore deeply
and unexpectedly into my teacher thinking when I enrolled in a summertime
professional development course at another university. Along with a group of
fellow teachers, I studied hard—all day.

One particular afternoon while engaged with a small group in intense discussion and writing, our teacher briskly circulated around the classroom
and told us to put away our materials because we were going on a field trip.
A complete surprise not listed on our course schedule, we clustered around
our teacher for a field trip to the unknown. He led us mysteriously through a
long underground tunnel that extended across campus and emerged in another university building, a fascinating historical museum resplendent with
the inventions of university alumni.

The inventor museum did not relate at all to the content of the course, and
we didn't care. It allowed us a meaningful break and an appreciative glimpse
into the talent produced by the university. Over the next half hour, we ambled
around the museum, stopping here and there to read and gaze at the fascinating displays. Unlike some taskmaster teachers who could have held us in class
with colorless facts, determined that we glean every last morsel of content, this
teacher surprised us with an incredibly enjoyable diversion. Returning later to
the classroom, we found that the brain break helped us refocus on our task
with more productive results.

TEACHING WITH PURPOSE

■ She had a talent for explaining concepts in a way that everyone understood. If we didn't, she patiently helped us grasp them and willingly stayed to give extra help. There needs to be more teachers like
this rather than ones who are just there with no purpose. (Abigail)

Teaching with purpose means that teachers take learning seriously, diversifying strategies and inventing unconventional strategies to engage all students. Our granddaughter Claire enjoyed an exceptional first-grade teacher who taught with purpose. Like most teachers, her prime purpose centered on student learning, but unlike ordinary teachers, she invented any creative or nontraditional strategy needed to accomplish her purpose, as she did with Claire.

Even at six years old, Claire had an active first-grade social calendar brimming with a cadre of loyal and spirited friends. As with all sociable children, Claire admitted to me that she often preferred chatting with her friends to doing her schoolwork. I asked Claire how she resolved this dilemma when she had no option but to dig in and complete her work. With dramatic flare, she demonstrated her teacher's unusual focusing strategy.

Unlike some teachers who resolutely demand attention or repeatedly scold social chitchat, Claire's teacher allowed her to sprawl flat on the floor, face down, under her table, to complete workbook assignments—admittedly, a bit unconventional. As Claire explained with theatrical gestures, "I have five sides to shield me when I do my work—the top of the table and the legs of the table. I can't see any of my friends, and so I do my work without talking. My teacher lets me do that sometimes—great, huh?" Claire's teacher is comfortable with classroom configurations that work for student learning—unconventional but purposeful.

An essential goal that purpose-driven teachers embrace is the goal of stimulating students to develop new ideas through critical thinking. As we have acknowledged in previous chapters, there is a place in schooling for memorizing facts and digesting the ideas of other people, but, more important, students must learn to think for themselves. Students who complain about "busywork" are voicing their frustration with the inordinate time allotted by some teachers for mundane tasks and tedious routines that suck the life from deep reflective thinking to develop ideas.

■ She believed in what she taught and who she taught. She shared herself and her knowledge, she didn't ask for memorization and busywork like some teachers, and she wanted us to form thoughts and ideas of our own and follow through with them. She made education what it should be in theory but rarely is—the development of ideas. (Jocelyn)

The development of ideas entails gathering information, analyzing it, making inferences, being open to new ways of considering old ideas, reflecting, comparing, contrasting, evaluating, and improving on previous opinions without becoming defensive about former ways of thinking.

When I engage students in critical thinking to develop their ideas, I find it well worth our time and effort. For example, I require students who are learning to teach to engage in an essential critical thinking task as they gradually move from students to apprentice classroom teachers. As they gradually acquire classroom teaching experience, they journal their thoughts on the process and develop their ideas—ideas that extend beyond their memories of the past and the excellent teachers they have encountered as students.

This critical thinking exercise must be more than a simple description of what they accomplished with a lesson plan. Rather, it must be an analysis of the decisions they made, how those decisions impacted the learning outcomes for students as a whole, and how their strategies worked for diverse students with special needs. They must further reflect on how each experience will inform their decisions for the next time they teach.

■ When I first came to the university, I had a hard time going to my classes because they were all long lectures and the teachers never noticed if we came or not, especially since they looked down at notes to lead the class. Second semester I had one of my greatest teachers. I admired him because he made it very clear that we were to attend every time, be caught up on our reading, and develop our ideas so as to participate in class discussion. Many professors have the attitude that we have made the decision to attend college and we must personally decide to go to class and learn. Not him. (Beverly)

TO RISK OR NOT TO RISK

Astute teachers dutifully attend to creating a classroom environment where students feel safe to take risks. All things considered, most students feel self-conscious about joining classroom discourse when they are uncertain about hanging their ideas out like laundry on a line for teachers and classmates to scrutinize and perhaps rip down. Even when student answers or ideas are dead wrong, by any stretch of the imagination, they want and need safety in offering and receiving.

■ He never made any of us feel stupid or inferior in any way. Sometimes teachers will say little things that make students feel dumb, but
he never did. He honestly tried to get everyone to understand him. At
the end of his presentation, he would ask if anyone had any questions. That class to this day is the only class I've ever been in where
no one was afraid to ask questions. (Jacob)

Nothing is more humiliating for students than when a teacher makes them
feel dumb, whether or not the derision is deliberate. I know. As a vulnerable
seventh grader with training-wheel self-esteem, I vividly remember a young
student teacher who taught my history class. I liked my regular teacher, so the
intrusion of a new teacher unsettled my thinking and challenged my orientation; nevertheless, at the time, I strived to impress him with my diligence and
knowledge.

As a teacher educator, I now have more insight about student teachers
than I did in seventh grade. I understand their inexperience and their desire
to be casual and funny in front of their classes, and I council them that humor must never be at the expense of a student's feelings. Back in seventh
grade, however, I grasped little of the purpose for having a "new" teacher that
semester, and I expected my student teacher to be the same as all my other
teachers. He was not.

This inexperienced student teacher made it his unstated aim to inject humor in every lesson, often at the expense of unsuspecting students. I remember one class period, in particular, when he maneuvered through his lesson
like a stand-up comedian, asking questions, pausing for student responses, or
answering his own questions with a weird metaphor or absurd conclusion intended to spark peels of teenage laughter.

As the lesson progressed, one of his questions captured my attention. I had
studied the topic carefully the night before, and sitting there at my desk, I had
an informed idea. I raised my hand, and when he did not immediately recognize me, I waved my hand higher and more vigorously. When he continued to
ignore me, I began bouncing subtly in my seat, voicing an emphatic "Oooh . . .
oooh," usually recognizable to discerning teachers as coming from a student
who knows the correct answer. Not to this teacher.

Unlike some teachers who might have at least smiled in my direction, this
student teacher belatedly acknowledged my eagerness with, "The bathroom is

down the hall, and you may go now." He chuckled with glee, and my peers followed suit. A shy and proper young lady, I felt embarrassed and dumb. I never again volunteered to share my intellectual contributions as long as he remained my teacher. Perhaps with experience, he settled into more appropriate and timely humor, but I still remember his insensitive, misplaced attempts to look cool at the expense of his students.

■ He treated us like we had a brain in our head, and he allowed us to take control of our own learning. He used some lecture, but a lot of our learning came about as he directed our questions and discussions. I believe he was a student as well, in some ways, because he asked our opinions, wondered how we solved certain problems, and supported our thinking. His classroom was safe enough that we felt like taking risks. (Amy)

SORTING TEACHERS

Students have expectations for teachers, and over their years of experience, as observers and recipients of all that teachers have to offer, students begin to sort teachers and teacher characteristics into categories—mediocre, exceptional, and everything in between. As students consider this collective group, they recognize that juxtaposed against a backdrop of ordinary teachers, their exceptional teachers stand out, illuminating the recesses of the classroom like a shining light in a dim space.

■ Looking back, I think that things started to go downhill for me educationally after fourth grade. Other teachers couldn't hold a candle to Mrs. M. (Lauren)

Such teachers don't turn off students or the classroom light by spewing facts, isolating themselves on a pedestal, or leaving students in the wayside darkness. Rather, they throw open the windows of learning, sharing the light and sparking curiosity and creativity. Such teachers possess a set of skills, an authenticity, and a depth of character that prompts them to suspend a teacher-only perspective on classroom life in favor of discerning the student perspective and seeking to meet their needs and expectations for the role of an excellent teacher. With the discerning there follows well-reasoned responses and decisions to the complexities they face.

Teaching is intricately dependent on human interaction, and those teachers who are sensitive to human interaction have more than intellectual expertise; they possess the emotional intelligence associated with insight, empathy, and compassion (Goleman 1995). Psychologist Haim Ginott (1972) points out that the wide psychological divide between teachers and students can be spanned through the practice of these emotional virtues in accurately responding to student needs. We would do well to preserve these "vanishing virtues" as sacred ideals in the classroom.

KEY IDEAS

✓ Student perceptions, whether fair or not, mirror their classroom reality.

✓ Reflecting on dramatic word images like *up on a pedestal, spewing facts,* or *left by the wayside* can remind teachers of characterizations to steadfastly avoid, juxtaposed with positive characterizations to emulate, like teaching with a purpose while discerning the perspective of students.

13

The Essence of Excellence

■ Overall I can't pinpoint exactly why everyone liked him so much, but it was and still is for certain that there is a line to get into his classes. (James)

THE EXCELLENCE JOURNEY

Educators have long pursued the essence of teacher excellence and the preparation route to attaining it, offering a wealth of useful and important ideas to ponder. One thing we have known for a long time: it is hard to be a teacher, and it is especially hard to be an excellent teacher. It takes years of experience for teachers to hone their ability to analyze classroom situations and student needs and to make accurate inferences and good decisions about how to proceed. Acquiring such skill takes dedication, authenticity, reflection, and perseverance (Berliner 1986; Lortie 2002; Darling-Hammond and Bransford 2005; Good and Brophy 2007).

As teachers and students, we have collectively logged a lot of hours in the classroom and experienced times of unsurpassed excellence, giving our best to teaching and learning, reveling when all unfolds as planned or better than dreamed. Mingled now and then among the extraordinary experiences, however, are the ordinary, tedious, even mediocre days in the classroom when even the best plans and intentions fall flat. Having encountered a full gamut of teachers and experiences, what, then, is the essence of excellence?

Like others, I am still learning and reflecting on the ideals of teacher excellence, striving along a journey that has a destination but no final stopping point. Along the route, teeming with detours and obstacles, I find it all too easy to lose sight of my focus on the big picture, the purposes of education, and the aspirations that define teacher excellence.

Together with fellow travelers, professional insight affords us vistas—clear-cut pathways to learn, reflect, and strive toward excellence. Among them are conferring with trusted colleagues who also strive, journaling at the end of a teaching day, reading the collective wisdom of research and practice, participating in the community, attending meaningful conferences, and amending classroom strategies—all worthy ventures for teacher travelers mapping the route to excellence.

The teacher perspective on excellence is essential, informative, and, if considered with care, restorative. Likewise, students, by virtue of their role as recipients and coauthors of classroom life, provide another unique perspective on teacher excellence. Their collective vista is illustrated throughout the pages in this book. I now circle back to the student perspective, to those students whose memories provided the impetus for me to reflect on my own journey as a teacher and observer of teaching. With hopes of packaging broad insights about excellent teachers, we will revisit several notable student memories and explore a few new ones.

A COMPOSITE OF EXCELLENCE

When students size up teachers, as James did in the opening vignette, what qualities and skills come across as so excellent, so intriguing, so inviting that students stand in line hoping to enroll in a particular class based, to a large extent, on the teacher? When a teacher excels, students know, they tell their parents, they tell other students, a stellar reputation grows and spreads, and the figurative line to get in the teacher's class extends long with anticipation and fervor.

■ His popularity was almost cultlike with some students. When you took one of his courses, you knew you were in for a fun yet informative class, unlike any other in the school. (Kyle)

In offering their perspective, students sorted teachers and then wrote intently, choosing to pedestal their most outstanding teachers, acting the role of potters each adding a handful of clay to a master teacher sculpture. And yet teachers are rightly so diverse, so gifted, and so unique in knowledge and experience that sculpting a composite teacher to honor excellence defies reality. At the very least, the idea of adequately or remotely capturing the essence of teacher excellence is daunting.

The task of excerpting student vignettes for this book in order to illustrate teachers and classroom life, across all grade levels and subject areas, sometimes left me with an out of context understanding of the essence of an excellent teacher from a student perspective. So, once again, I assembled all 148 handwritten essays and read them in context in one sitting.

The students wrote eloquently about real people, teachers with names, minds, talents, and dreams for themselves as teachers and for their students as learners. The teachers succeeded wildly, and students characterized them as excellent. In reading the essays again, I challenged myself to pare all the episodes, characterizations, qualities, and skills and distill them to the most basic composite of an excellent teacher.

I envisioned broadly an elementary, middle school, high school, or college teacher, male or female, representing any subject area, and I share the essence as reflective, not definitive. I considered all the handwritten student memories, each filled with meaningful episodes, and reduced them to what rang true to my experience. Somewhere beyond one hundred essays, I began to glimpse the master sculpture and formed a simple one-sentence inscription honoring excellent teachers: an excellent teacher is personally lighthearted and caring while simultaneously serious about teaching and learning.

At first glance, the words depict a dichotomy—lighthearted and serious—opposite characteristics but the same person. It beckons a closer look. Among the student essays, I discovered a vivid composite, not yet shared, that illuminated my thinking on the essence of an excellent teacher. The same description could apply to any excellent teacher, male or female, at any grade level, who represents any subject area.

■ Every day he came to class with a smile. But more importantly, he truly cared about his students and his job performance. He was lighthearted, making the classroom environment an enjoyable one, but he was serious toward teaching and learning. He had a good heart—a smile that separated him from the rest—and he showed us the joy that could be found in teaching. (Joseph)

Consider the four elements embodied in the description: lighthearted, caring, serious about teaching, and serious about learning. The first two words speak to the personal qualities of excellent teachers, and the last two phrases speak to the important work of excellent teachers.

These four universal elements in no way obscure a teacher's individual personality or authenticity. On the contrary, when embraced, these elements act as core principles through which to function effectively as unique, individual teachers. What do the words *lighthearted* and *caring* and the phrases *serious about teaching* and *serious about learning* imply for teachers who wish to make a difference in the classroom?

PERSONALLY LIGHTHEARTED

The realization of lightheartedness, as a personal quality of excellence, stirred my thinking to a greater degree than did the other three more customary elements of teaching excellence. Lightheartedness was not a specific quality I had typically seen on lists of "excellent teacher qualities" lauded by teacher educators, but as I reread the entire collection of 148 essays in one sitting, a recurring thought about these outstanding teachers seeped into my consciousness—these people are happy, relaxed, confident, vital, optimistic, and easy to be around. If I had the opportunity, I knew that I would enjoy their company as valued colleagues.

The term *lighthearted*, as I came to embrace it, does not imply a Pollyanna approach to life. Lighthearted teachers are not unmindful of the challenges in their classrooms, the school, the community, or the world, but they refuse to be downtrodden by them. Daily stresses and tensions have little visible impact. These teachers refuse to take classroom irritations personally or themselves too seriously. Rather, they approach life, especially classroom life, as optimists.

Lighthearted teachers relish their calling to the classroom where they unroll energy, enthusiasm, and joy, spreading it around contagiously. I envision vibrant eyes and congenial smiles, indications of teachers who revel in the company of students and the back-and-forth connections a good relationship affords.

■ He loved being in the classroom with "his" kids. He loved seeing our minds develop. He loved watching us grow, and he loved being a part of it all. He loved to teach; it was evident to all of us, even as seventh graders. (Jacob)

UNCONDITIONAL CARING

The word *caring* conveys a deeply ingrained personal attitude. Some might suggest that excellent teachers are born with this characteristic, radiating a caring disposition in the classroom with little effort. But more to the point, excellent teachers cultivate caring as a core attitude, and educators have long honored this quality as essential and nourishing for students.

Coupled with a lighthearted nature, caring teachers deeply respect and love their students unconditionally, not as one obliged by a paycheck. Caring teachers encircle all students, equally respecting those who reciprocate and those who do not, those who eagerly and cooperatively engage, and those who, for whatever reason, come with quirky, irksome, even surly dispositions that can try the patience of the most caring teacher.

I once visited a first-grade room where I immediately noticed a boy with long, moppish hair and rather disheveled clothing poking the neatly coifed, smartly put-together boy beside him, attempting to lure the boy's attention away from their teacher. When it didn't work, the mischievous child planted his eyes and nose a mere two inches from his classmate's eyes and nose and commenced an animated, albeit one-sided conversation. Meanwhile, the gracious and caring teacher gently repositioned the misbehaving student, maintaining her vivacious smile and continuing her lesson unfettered by the distraction.

A few minutes later, as the students transitioned from their seats to a new activity, the same restless boy jumped up like a jackrabbit and somersaulted across the front of the room. The gracious teacher, without missing a beat, corralled the student, enveloped him closely, gently, and proceeded to enlist his help in some spur-of-the-moment task while moving ahead with the class activity, a compassionate smile still on her face.

Sitting there, as a stunned visitor watching this play out, I was awed by the teacher's unconditional regard and consistent caring efforts for this child. I had only one recurring thought—God bless this woman. She certainly has her hands full with this kid. But what did I know about this first grader? Absolutely nothing. It was tempting—no, all too easy—to size up this child in a snapshot observation. Later, I learned the poignant and heartbreaking truth; the boy's mother had died of cancer the previous year and he had been shuttled endlessly between relatives ever since.

Caring is a choice, independent of circumstances but ever sensitive to context. It entails seeing students, really seeing students, understanding their vulnerabilities, and guarding them fiercely from threats to their fragile human nature. In order to really see students, caring teachers find ways to purposefully connect with students by circulating through the classroom, listening, answering questions, and affirming. Unconditional caring lets students know that they are respected just because they exist, even when they neglect their schoolwork or disrupt the class.

■ She didn't reveal her caring side freely, but later, I went back to visit, and she became my friend. That's when I realized how deeply she always cared for students in trying to teach us about "life after high school." When she left her job, I helped her pack up her room—her life, as she said. Wherever she is today, I love her as a dear friend. (Jade)

SERIOUS ABOUT TEACHING

Lighthearted and caring teacher qualities do not detract from the serious nature and ethical work carried out in the classroom; on the contrary, such qualities invite students to the business of learning. Skilled teachers seamlessly weave lighthearted and caring personal qualities with a steadfast, responsible mind-set on teaching. They take their responsibility to prepare seriously.

■ He was an avid researcher, and it showed in his lectures. Every lecture was loaded with information, and I walked away with pages of notes. You could just tell he was about to burst as he talked since he had so much to say about everything. His research showed as he talked; he wrote book titles on the board attributing ideas to various authors. (Steven)

On several occasions, I have invited a guest speaker, an excellent and highly experienced high school teacher, to share her insights with my students preparing for high school teaching careers. Strong, principled, and confident, she never failed to inspire my students and get me revved up as well.

Nestled among her wise firsthand advice was a point she nailed down repeatedly, her mantra delivered with passion and resolve, "Don't ever, ever wing it; teaching is your job." And she walked the talk despite being a veteran teacher, nearing retirement. I admired that about her. Visiting her classroom, unannounced on several occasions, I noted her unique style of color coded lesson plans neatly and simply arranged on three-by-five-inch cards, freshly revised with each new school year.

The best teachers avoid a hodgepodge of last-minute, thrown-together lessons tossed at students with hopes that something will stick. Instead, no matter how they choose to consider and organize the endless details of classroom life, excellent teachers take their job seriously; they plan.

SERIOUS ABOUT LEARNING

Teachers who are laser focused on student learning spend time and energy considering ways to motivate and harness student preferences and potential, believing in students enough to support their fledgling efforts with diverse strategies, needed assistance, specific encouragement, and expectations for success.

Of the four elements of teaching excellence put forth here, student learning is probably the most challenging to figure out and get consistently right. That doesn't stop excellent teachers from working at it, exploring its nuances, taking it seriously. Classes are challenging but fair, purposes are clear and explicit, and assessments are varied and meaningful.

I can say unequivocally that in all 148 essays about excellent teachers, not one characterized a class as easy. On the contrary, teachers made no apologies for expecting students to learn, and with a sincere belief and message that all students can learn, coupled with fair and consistent teacher support, students responded. Excellent teachers are learning leaders.

■ It was apparent that she worked hard as a teacher, and we were expected to work hard as students. We felt like a team, like we were each special and important to the class—like we really belonged. When I say "we," I'm speaking for myself as well as many other members of the class who expressed similar opinions. The most important thing I can say, that I can't say about many, is that I learned what I needed to learn and gained the background necessary for further learning. (Mia)

The composite essence of an excellent teacher as personally lighthearted and caring while simultaneously serious about teaching and learning applies consistently for teachers at all grade levels from kindergarten through college. These four elements are universal in their call to excellence.

Although there is considerable overlap, excellence manifests in subtly different ways across grade levels. Some of the differences relate to students' developmental needs. For example, younger students depend on their teachers to jump-start basic skill practice and provide creative surroundings, older students rely on teachers to support their developing and sometimes rocky self-image, and young adult students expect teachers to inspire deep thought and foster career aspirations. Consider, briefly, the nuances of excellence across grade levels.

ELEMENTARY TEACHERS

■ As you entered our classroom, you instantly felt relaxed. Student writings and art projects decorated the walls and hung from the ceiling. We always had several live animals in our room (hamsters, guinea pigs, fish, and birds, all at one time!). This was great. I loved this because it gave us, as students, a sense of ownership of the classroom. (Jennifer)

Elementary children make their first formal foray into the world of teachers and students with unbridled enthusiasm. I love to hear their unsullied descriptions. As I write, our grandson, Jack, is readying to attend school for the first time. He telephoned the other night to describe his orientation visit. "My teacher is real nice! They have instruments at school, and you can pick any instrument you want to play. They have a stage at school for us to do programs. You can go outside or inside or do anything at school. And they have a bathroom at school."

Youngsters, yet to enroll for the first time, repeat the word *school* often, with awe and wonder. School, the big building shrouded in an aura of mystery, looms impressively like a hallowed place of dreams and possibility, gaining significance as opening day approaches. Elementary teachers relish the innocent enthusiasm of young children untarnished by cynical veterans of school life.

As the first to introduce children to all that the word *school* entails, elementary teachers have perhaps the most sacred responsibility of all teachers to set the tone for student attitudes about education, attitudes that extend for years. Excellent elementary teachers establish structure, fostering early work habits, goal setting, and self-regulation. They make certain that students develop basic skills, and they persistently establish appropriate leadership while caring almost like surrogate parents.

- She cared about all of us. When we had news, she let us share it with the class. If someone was upset, she did something nice, like give you a note or let you be first in line. She was very into reading, and she helped us make goals for ourselves. We wrote our goals for the month on slips of paper, and she kept them. We got them back a month later. This taught me a lot about working toward an outcome. (Emily)

MIDDLE SCHOOL TEACHERS

Middle school teachers not only help students transition out of elementary school but also gingerly help students steer toward the adolescence highway without crashing. It's a heavy responsibility. Along the way, teachers know that middle school students are exasperating but delightful, growing exponentially while harboring the last vestiges of childhood, fearful of the unknown, longing to feel accepted and competent. Revisiting the following geography lesson from an earlier chapter offers a window into the needs and fears of middle school students as they cautiously step out of childhood.

- On the first day of class he introduced us to the basic elements of geography—latitude, longitude, and so on. He took an apple out of his pocket and started to peel it with a Swiss army knife. As he worked with the apple, he discussed the shape of the earth (round) and its crust (like the peel). He sliced the apple and asked questions aloud. All of us were shy and quiet because it was the first day of class in the big middle school. I tentatively raised my hand and answered his question, "Latitude?" "Right," he said, and handed me the first apple slice. I felt really smart that day. (Ava)

Once acquainted and settled into a new school year, middle school teachers and their students enjoy a decidedly new level of fun. I suspect this is because middle school students are still young enough to be somewhat in awe of a teacher but old enough to cleverly engage teachers in lighthearted jests. In fact, I have had a number of students prepare to teach high school with absolutely no thought of teaching in middle school—that is, until they have completed a middle school field experience and discovered how much fun these kids can be.

I once visited a middle school specifically to participate with the students in their cooperative learning adventures. My group of five cooperative classmates expected my arrival, welcomed me to their table, and playfully introduced themselves. "My name is Jennifer," the confident sixth grader nodded my way as she took a seat at the large round table where I was already sitting with two other students. "Hi Jennifer," I smiled and patted her arm. "That's not her real name," countered her tablemate chuckling. Bemused, Jennifer shrugged. "My name is really Sarah." Exposed, we laughed as she grinned at me mischievously.

Sarah wore a trendy skirt, small earrings, lots of lip gloss, and a faint dusting of glitter across her face. She appeared older than her eleven years. I marveled at how quickly middle school students can shed childhood like yesterday's cocoon.

Middle school students try on different names and persona as they figure out who they might like to become. Middle school teachers navigate these classrooms, filled with chameleon students, skillfully and gracefully. They see students, behind the facade, and help them discover their talents, seeking their preferences and encouraging their potential. Good teachers maintain that middle school is not a holding tank of hormones but a place for students to explore a broader view of life and their emerging place in it.

■ My middle school teacher was an exceptional lady. She somehow made every student want to achieve and believe in themselves. She was pleasant and enthusiastic about the subjects she taught. She made people and events become real in the classroom. I thought she was the best teacher ever. (Maria)

HIGH SCHOOL TEACHERS

While middle school students begin a decided transition to adolescence, high school students churn through a brain and identity overhaul that needs meticulous care by caring teachers. By nature, high schools are often large and impersonal, and this works at odds with a commitment to caring about students as individuals. Herding several thousand students lockstep through a cookie-cutter high school experience won't enhance their growth, confidence, or inclination to learn. Although high school students are reticent to acknowledge it, they crave the unbridled interest and validation that excellent teachers offer.

■ She was the first teacher who I felt saw me as a person—an independent entity—and not part of a group or a teenager or an adolescent—but as a person who had something to give her. (Jocelyn)

As a former high school teacher, I understand the temptation to mentally lasso students into categories, labeled efficiently rather than noticed individually. I recall one of my high school students, a vital member of the soccer team, a student whom I reluctantly excused from class after class for "away" games. It was tempting to label him a jock, interested primarily in sports, a myopic, narrow-minded view of a student athlete.

One day, however, I noticed a camera peeking out of his backpack, a rather nice camera at that. Being an amateur but respectable photographer myself, I gestured toward his backpack and asked about the camera. Charmed by my interest, he proceeded to haul out his full camera equipment and detail his passion and considerable talent for photography. Our rapt conversation was a far cry from the soccer field, affording me a new dimension from which to appreciate this student.

Students who morph through turbulent teenage years appreciate high school teachers who attend to them as individuals, rejecting the usual category stamp. It doesn't take long to show interest, a few minutes here and there, before class, after school, whenever. Savvy teachers look for fleeting opportunities to validate students, and in a large high school or any high school, it means a lot.

When it comes to learning, excellent high school teachers have high expectations, and classes can be intense as teachers prepare students for their next step—college, vocational school, or life on the job. Wise high school teachers allow students some flexibility and choice in what they study and how they demonstrate learning. At the same time, these teachers instill a love of the subject, often sprinkling it with well-placed humor. In the end, students characteristically refer to an excellent high school teacher as a friend, a mentor.

■ She was an absolutely incredible high school teacher. Her class was challenging yet fun. I think her greatest asset was that she had a wonderful sense of humor, and she knew how to joke around with a room full of sixteen-year-olds. Her lectures were clear and full of examples that usually had some humor behind them or an interesting story. She was respected because she was fair. Her class was very hard, but she was available for special help. You wanted to do well; you wanted her to be proud of you because she genuinely cared about her students. She was a friend, a truly memorable educator! (Leslie)

COLLEGE TEACHERS

After twelve or more years of education, college students have amassed a lot of information and experience. Many have decided their career path, and they are on a mission to pursue it. As such, college students are less tolerant of mundane busywork than students at other grade levels might be. What college students do want are teachers who give them more than they can glean unilaterally from textbooks.

Excellent college teachers focus on that need, teaching far beyond the text from a depth and breadth of experience, supplementing with examples, research, film clips, models, maps, and primary resources. In so doing, inspiring college teachers can deliver eloquent presentations because their passion and enthusiasm for the subject subsumes a more scripted, yawning college lecture.

■ One of his most admirable assets was his knowledge of the subject matter. He walked around before our class and never looked at any notes. He spoke about the subject with expertise and enthusiasm. My confidence in his being an authority on the material made me want to learn it. (Beverly)

Good college teachers recognize that their students often have extensive prior knowledge and practical experience with topics under discussion. Students, eager to play active roles, engage their diverse experiences to make meaningful contributions to class discussions. They prefer an application-based analysis of topics rather than abstract theories and explanations. In short, they abhor spoon-feeding.

I continue to marvel at my university students—their background, areas of interest, and levels of expertise. In a recent course, one of my university students wowed me with stories from her work as a figure skating teacher, likewise capturing the attention and input of the entire class. Having nearly made an Olympics ice skating team, this student turned her considerable expertise into an admirable career working with young Olympic hopefuls.

She cleverly threaded her broad knowledge and out of the ordinary teaching experience into our class discussions about motivation, precision, perseverance, and assessment. We all gained new insights from her. More and more, I discover that it is not just the teacher who holds the keys to knowledge, understanding, and application.

COMPLEX RESPONSIBILITY

Teachers, at every grade level, shoulder a complex responsibility. What students see and experience in the classroom is a small measure of a teacher's role, like a shovel of sand on a far-reaching seashore. Teachers hold much in their minds and hearts, more than what is on display for students and others to see. They embody a wealth of preparation, practice, knowledge, experience, compassion, and dreams for their students.

If, as suggested in this chapter, an excellent teacher blends a lighthearted demeanor with unconditional caring while simultaneously maintaining a serious focus on teaching and learning, how is that complex blending engineered by teachers, behind the scenes, to be accomplished, successfully, in the classroom with students? What is a teacher's unseen work?

Excellent teachers spend a great deal of time thinking about their students and preparing lessons and activities. All told, teachers spend more time thinking and preparing than they do teaching, as much as two or three times more. Ever before a teacher looms the prospect of the next lesson, the profound diversity of student needs, and the purposeful speculation on how to coordinate the two successfully. Unseen by students, a teacher's mind teems with numerous questions that swirl like ingredients in a blender with no off button. What follows is a mere sampling of those behind-the-scenes teacher questions.

How should I introduce the topic? What if I'm met with blank expressions? What prior knowledge do students have, and how can I tap into it? How can I make sure that students understand the relationship between their prior knowledge and the new topic? What kind of review will students need first?

What is going on right now with students outside the classroom? What is their mood, their burdens, their joys? How will I relate, be sensitive, and probe, if necessary, without being intrusive? Have they had breakfast and a hug this morning? Are they ready to learn?

Will the lesson include a key concept? If so, how can I teach the concept so that students will grasp it solidly enough to support later learning? Should I present the topic step-by-step? Should I organize cooperative groups? How can I maximize learning preferences? How can I avoid tedium and sustain interest? Am I in a rut?

How will students respond when I raise certain questions? Where should I explain at length, and where should I encourage students to grapple with questions on their own? What can I expect the advanced students to learn from this lesson? What can I expect the average students to learn or the students who need more time? What if students are disinclined to engage? How can I differentiate instruction to reach and motivate them?

How will students demonstrate their learning? What choices can I offer? When is the next standardized test coming along? How will I prepare students in a meaningful way without losing my focus on the larger goals of education? And, in the end, how can I set the stage for students to learn the next concept and for related concepts they will encounter in the future?

It is one thing for teachers to prepare the content and another thing for teachers to know their students. If teachers intertwine the two together effectively, they succeed. Teachers think about these two things—the content and the students—over and over. It seems simple, but when teachers do it well, it is complicated and subtle and takes a lot of time.

Students do not understand all that goes into teaching. They aren't privy to the backstory, only the recipients of its results, and they know excellence when they see and experience it. Still, students may not fully appreciate their teachers until years later when students reflect on classroom memories and recognize the depth of preparation and mentoring they have received.

It's funny how teachers are the last to know about their students' memories and reflections, like my third-grade teacher, Mrs. Houghton, who never knew how much I later appreciated her influence on my life and career choice. Likewise, the teachers highlighted in student memories throughout this book likely knew little of how students collectively appreciated their efforts and care.

And so to you who are teachers and students of teaching, if you see your highest aspirations, best qualities, sound strategies, and strong relationships paralleled somewhere in this book, be assured that you, too, are making a difference in the classroom and in the lives of students.

■ Upon returning to visit her class a couple of years ago, she affirmed my faith in teachers by saying, "This is the best class I have ever had," which is the same thing she told my class many years ago. Things just keep getting better and better! (Nicholas)

AN ENDURING LEGACY

In his infamous *Last Lecture*, Carnegie Mellon professor Randy Pausch delivered his last lesson and legacy in an hour-long lecture later seen by millions online. Despite a diagnosis of terminal pancreatic cancer, Pausch lightheartedly unfolded his teacher wit and wisdom several months before he passed away. With unflagging optimism for life and compassion for his students, he reminded them to keep their childhood dreams alive, embrace hard work, and remember that "luck is where preparation meets opportunity" (Pausch, 2008, 119).

Consistently and without fanfare, excellent teachers, in their own authentic and unique way, create a splendid and enduring legacy through the many students they shepherd through their classrooms. Although modestly compensated by most standards, teachers who make a difference in the classroom and in students' lives are among the truly wealthy. These teachers, at all grade levels, leave a priceless inheritance for all of us: they leave generations of educated people who make a difference in the world.

KEY IDEAS

✓ Lighthearted teachers permeate the classroom with energy and joy.

✓ Caring teachers nourish students unconditionally, even those who don't reciprocate.

✓ Responsible teachers are steadfast in the work of preparation; they don't wing it.

✓ Excellent teachers are serious about learning, they believe that all students can learn, and they travel in the trenches with each student in the process.

References

Armstrong, T. (2000). *Multiple intelligences in the classroom* (2nd ed.). Alexandria, VA: Association of Supervision and Curriculum Development.

Atkinson, R., & Shiffrin, R. (1968). Human memory: A proposed system and its control processes. In K. Spence & J. Spence (Eds.), *The psychology of learning and motivation: Advances in research and theory.* New York: Academic Press.

Ayers, W. (2001). *To teach: The journey of a teacher* (2nd ed.). New York: Teachers College Press.

Balli, S. J., Demo, D. H., & Wedman, J. F. (1998). Family involvement with children's homework: An intervention in the middle grades. *Family Relations, 47*(2), 149–157.

Berliner, D. (1986). In pursuit of the expert pedagogue. *Educational Researcher, 15*(7), 5–13.

Biddle, B. J. (1979). *Role theory: Expectations, identities, and behaviors.* New York: Academic Press.

Bruner, J. (1960). *The process of education.* Cambridge, MA: Harvard University Press.

Burstein, A. (1995). *The inner Jefferson.* Charlottesville: University Press of Virginia.

Cameron, J. (Producer/Director), & Landau (Producer). (1997). *Titanic* [Motion picture]. United States: Twentieth Century-Fox.

Campbell, S. (1955). *Fiddlesticks and Freckles.* Indianapolis, IN: Bobbs-Merrill.

Can Bill Gates fix our failing schools? (2007, September 23). *Parade,* 23.

Canter, L., & Canter, M. (2001). *Assertive discipline* (3rd ed.). Bloomington, IN: Solution Tree.

Carson, B. (2006). *Think big: Unleashing your potential for excellence.* Grand Rapids, MI: Zondervan Publishing House.

Clark, M. (2005). *Juxtapositions: Ideas for college writers.* Boston: Pearson Custom Publishing.

Clark, R. (2004a). *The excellent 11: Qualities teachers and parents use to motivate, inspire, and educate children.* New York: Hyperion.

Clark, R. (2004b). *The essential 55: An award-winning educator's rules for discovering the successful student in every child.* New York: Hyperion.

Collins, M., & Tamarkin, C. (1990). *Marva Collins' way: Returing to excellence in education.* New York: Penguin Putnam.

Cooper, H. (2007). *The battle over homework: Common ground for administrators, teachers, and parents* (3rd ed.). Thousand Oaks, CA: Corwin Press.

Crabb, L. J., & Allender, D. B. (1984). *Encouragement: The key to caring.* Grand Rapids, MI: Zondervan.

Craik, F., & Lockhart, R. (1972). Levels of processing: A framework for memory research. *Journal of Verbal Thinking and Verbal Behavior, 11,* 671–684.

Cushman, P. (2005). It's just not a real bloke's job: Male teachers in the primary school. *Asia Pacific Journal of Teacher Education, 33*(3), 321–338.

Dale, E. (1969). *Audio-visual methods in teaching* (3rd ed.). New York: Holt, Rinehart and Winston.

Darling-Hammond, L., & Bransford, J. (Eds.). (2005). *Preparing teachers for a changing world.* San Francisco: Jossey-Bass.

Dee, T. S. (2006). The why chromosome. *Education Next, 6*(4), 68–75.

Dewey, J. (1916). *Democracy and education: An introduction to the philosophy of education.* London: Macmillan.

Dosa, D. M. (2007). A day in the life of Oscar the cat. *New England Journal of Medicine, 357*(4), 328–329.

Festinger, L. (1957). *A theory of cognitive dissonance.* Stanford, CA: Stanford University Press.

Gardner, H. (1983). *Frames of mind: The theory of multiple intelligences.* New York: Basic Books.

Gardner, H. (1991). *The unschooled mind.* New York: Basic Books.

Garner, R. (2005). Humor, analogy, and metaphor: H.A.M. it up in teaching. *Radical Pedagogy, 6*(2), 1.

George, J. C. (1972). *Julie of the wolves.* New York: HarperCollins.

Ginott, H. (1972). *Teacher and child: A book for parents and teachers.* New York: Avon Books.

Glasser, W. (1998). *The quality school.* New York: HarperCollins.

Glasser, W. (2000). *Every student can succeed.* Chatsworth, CA: William Glasser.

Goleman, D. (1995). *Emotional intelligence.* New York: Bantam Books.

Good, T. L., & Brophy, J. E. (2007). *Looking in classrooms* (10th ed.). Columbus, OH: Allyn & Bacon/Merrill Education.

Good, T. L., & Nichols, S. L. (2001). Expectancy effects in the classroom: A special focus on improving the reading performance of minority students in first-grade classrooms. *Educational Psychologist, 36,* 113–126.

Guillaume, A. M. (2008). *K–12 classroom teaching: A primer for new professionals.* Upper Saddle River, NJ: Pearson.

Henley, M. (2006). *Classroom management: A proactive approach.* Upper Saddle River, NJ: Pearson Education.

Hunter, M. (1982). *Mastery teaching.* Thousand Oaks, CA: Corwin Press.

Hyde, J. S., Lindberg, S. M., Linn, M. C., Ellis, A. B., & Williams, C. C. (2008). Gender similarities characterize math performance. *Science, 321*(5888), 494–495.

Jaquet, L. (Director). (2005). *March of the penguins.* [Motion picture]. United States: Warner Independent Films.

Johnson, S., & Johnson, C. (1986). *The one minute teacher.* New York: William Morrow.

Johnson, D. W., Johnson, R. T., & Holubec, E. J. (2007). *The nuts and bolts of cooperative learning* (2nd ed.). Edina, MN: Interaction Book Company.

King, K., & Gurian, M. (2006). Teaching to the minds of boys. *Educational Leadership, 64*(1), 56–61.

Klonoski, R. J. (2003). Teaching as a primordial act of friendship. *Journal of Educational Thought, 37*(2), 137–155.

Knowles, T., & Brown, D. F. (2007). *What every middle school teacher should know* (2nd ed.). Portsmouth, NH: Heinemann.

Kohn, A. (1999). *Punished by rewards: The trouble with gold stars, incentive plans, A's, praise, and other bribes.* Boston: Houghton Mifflin.

Kounin, J. S. (1970). *Discipline and group management in classrooms.* New York: Holt, Rinehart and Winston.

Kronowitz, E. L. (2008). *The teacher's guide to success.* Boston: Allyn & Bacon.

Lawrence-Lightfoot, S. (2000). *Respect.* New York: HarperCollins.

Liston, D., Whitcomb, J., & Borko, H. (2006). Too little or too much: Teacher preparation and the first years of teaching. *Journal of Teacher Education, 57*(4), 351–358.

Lortie, D. (2002). *Schoolteacher* (2nd ed.). Chicago: University of Chicago Press.

Marzano, R. J. (2003). *What works in schools.* Alexandria, VA: Association for Supervision and Curriculum Development.

National Association for Single Sex Public Education. (2008). Retrieved August 16, 2008, from http://www.singlesexschools.org

National Education Association. (2008). *Wanted: More male teachers.* Retrieved August 16, 2008, from http://www.nea.org/teachershortage

Pausch, R. (2008). *The last lecture.* New York: Hyperion.

Peck, M. S. (1978). *The road less traveled.* New York: Simon and Schuster.

Plaut, S. M. (1993). Boundary issues in teacher-student relationships. *Journal of Sex and Marital Therapy, 19,* 210–219.

Pollak, J. P., & Freda, P. D. (1997). Humor, learning, and socialization in middle level classrooms. *The Clearing House, 70,* 176–178.

Ponterotto, J. G., Utsey, S. O., & Pedersen, P. B. (2006). *Preventing prejudice: A guide for counselors, educators, and parents* (2nd ed.). Thousand Oaks, CA: Sage.

Popham, W. J. (2007). Report cards, test gaps, and item types. *Educational Leadership, 65*(2), 87–88.

Rosenblum-Lowden, R. (2000). *You have to go to school—You're the teacher.* Thousand Oaks, CA: Corwin Press.

Rosenthal, R., & Jacobson, L. (1968). *Pygmalion in the classroom: Teacher expectation and pupils intellectual development.* New York: Rinehart and Winston.

Ryan, R. M., & Deci, E. L. (2006). Self-regulation and the problem of human autonomy: Does psychology need choice, self-determination, and will? *Journal of Personality, 74*(6), 1157–1586.

Sadker, M. P., & Sadker D. (1994). *Failing at fairness: How our schools cheat girls.* New York: Touchstone.

Stowe, H. B. (1852). *Uncle Tom's cabin or life among the lowly.* New York: Vintage Books.

Stronge, J. H. (2002). *Qualities of effective teachers.* Alexandria, VA: Association for Supervision and Curriculum Development.

Tauber, R. T., & Mester, C. S. (2006). *Acting lessons for teachers: Using performance skills in the classroom* (2nd ed.). Westport, CT: Praeger.

Tomlinson, C. A. (2001). *How to differentiate instruction in mixed-ability classrooms.* (2nd ed.). Alexandria, VA: Association for Supervision and Curriculum Development.

U.S. Department of Education, National Center for Education Statistics. (2008). *Teacher distribution by gender 2003–2004.* Retrieved August 14, 2008, from http://nces.ed.gov

University of Missouri–Columbia, College of Education (2007). Boys can cry. *Ed Life.*

Weiner, B. (1986). *An attributional theory of motivation and emotion.* New York: Springer-Verlag.

White, E. B. (2002). *Charlotte's web* (50th anniversary ed.). New York: HarperCollins.

Wong, H. K., & Wong, R. T. (1998). *The first days of school.* Mountain View, CA: Harry K. Wong Publications.

About the Author

Sandra J. Balli pursued her love of teaching at an early age while playing school with neighborhood friends. She later earned a bachelor's degree in secondary education and home economics from Andrews University and went on to teach at a variety of grade levels. In 1995, she earned a PhD in curriculum and instruction from the University of Missouri–Columbia.

Sandy is currently an associate professor of education at La Sierra University in Riverside, California, where she teaches courses in middle school methods, advanced instructional models, and qualitative research. Sandy has published articles in numerous journals, including the *Journal of Experimental Education*, the *Journal of Research and Development in Education, Family Relations*, the *Journal of Continuing Higher Education, Principal, Educational Technology*, and the *Educational Forum*.